CONTENTS

Foreword

ManKind is a book that places great emphasis on the recognition that in order to make a peaceful world it is necessary to start by discovering our own inner peace, through faith, joy, love, prayer and meditation.

ManKind includes various Torah sources, and a collection of insightful and inspiring essays and quotes from spiritual leaders and academics that are aimed at helping us unlock ever deeper levels of our hidden potential, in the light of realizing the reality that we are all made in the image of our Creator.

Heralding the wonderful fulfillment of ancient Hebrew prophecy, ManKind explains how it is through an illuminated humanity energized with the joy of self-knowledge that our world will live in peace.

ManKind envisions the thriving, sustainable and caring world that will be ushered in with the dawning of the promised Messianic Age.

Including gems of wisdom and consciousness-raising exercises by such luminaries as the Lubavitcher Rebbe, Rebbe Nachman, Rabbi Aryeh Kaplan and Rabbi Shlomo Carlebach, ManKind offers a mind-blowing vision of the kind and joyful world the Almighty always wanted us to live in – which is within our grasp if we desire it enough.

"We must study the Torah looking upon it as a Book given us by the Almighty that we may learn from it to know what we are and what we should be in our earthly existence. It must be to us Torah, *that is, a source of instruction and guidance in the Almighty's world, a generator of spiritual life within us. We must ask ourselves, 'What will human beings be who recognize the contents of this Book as the rule of life given them by the Almighty?' "*

Rabbi Samson Raphael Hirsch in The Nineteen Letters

ManKind

A Spiritual Guide To
Making a World of Difference

A selection of inspiring quotes and essays to further self-realization and advance global transformation

Compiled by Nachum Shaw

Promised Land

JERUSALEM   LONDON   NEW YORK

For further information:

Promised Land Publishers

Apt. 8, 5 Gimmel Alroyi St.

Jerusalem 9210808

ISRAEL

or

Promised Land Publishers

8 Woodville Road

London NW11 9TN

ENGLAND

or

Promised Land Publishers

67 Wood Hollow Lane

New Rochelle

NY 10804

USA

Email: promisedland920@gmail.com

www.promisedlandpublishers.com

INTRODUCTION

"Developing a love for kindness transforms your life as you transform the lives of others. Kindness is one of the pillars of the world. Every act of kindness elevates your character and makes you a kinder person. As you continue to increase your love for kindness, you increase the amount of joy in your life.

There are minor acts of kindness and major acts of kindness. Every kind deed and word is precious and valuable. Every kind word and deed is eternal. And when your actions and words have a positive lifetime effect on someone, you have created something magnificent, whether or not the extent of its greatness is recognized by any other mortal.

As you expand your consciousness, you create a more spiritual life. Your kindness and compassion for the Creator's children is an expression of your love for our Father, our King, Creator and Sustainer of the universe. With your kindness and compassion you emulate Him. As you help others, you create an inner light that illuminates your entire being.

A master artist looks at an entirely different world than someone who lacks his vision. We can all train ourselves to see more deeply. When you see the world as a place in which to do kindness, you see a different world. You see a world full of spiritual opportunities wherever you are and wherever you go. Let this be your world."

RABBI ZELIG PLISKIN

In his book *To Heal a Fractured World*, Rabbi Jonathan Sacks writes, "The sociologist Peter Berger calls humour a 'signal of transcendence'. He wrote a book about it called *Redeeming Laughter,* emphasizing its religious dimension. A joke, he said, is a 'vignette of salvation'. Humour is at its most intense among persecuted peoples. It is the weapon of the weak against the strong. What we can laugh at, momentarily, we do not fear. I once wrote that I could not go all the way with Robert Benigni who made a comedy about the Holocaust and called it *Life is Beautiful.* Its theme was that, in otherwise unbearable circumstances, humour keeps us sane. I argued that in Auschwitz, humour might have kept you sane but it would not have kept you alive. I was corrected by an Auschwitz survivor. He told me that in the camp, he and a fellow prisoner made a point of finding one thing each day about which they could laugh. That, he said, was what kept us alive. I was wrong, and acknowledge the fact.

Humour is the oldest form of cognitive therapy, Jewish humour in particular lives in its ability at the last moment, to get us to see things differently, to reframe (it is no coincidence that Ludwig Wittgenstein, a philosopher of Jewish background, said that 'a philosophical work could be written entirely in the form of jokes'). Humour gives us a way out from what, until the last line, seemed an impossible situation. What we can laugh at, we can rise above. Humour is an assertion of humanity in the face of dehumanizing influences. It is a way of breaking the grip of fears that would otherwise hold us captive. It is, in its way, one of the supreme expressions of human freedom…freedom as the ability to redefine our situation. Those who can laugh at fate, redeem it from tragedy. One who rejects his enemy's interpretation of events cannot be made a victim. Psychologically, he or she remains free. Humour is the first cousin of hope."

Despite all the terrible suffering, exiles, persecutions and mass murder that the Jewish people have been subject to, amazingly, they carried on believing in G-d, yearning and praying every day for Jerusalem to be rebuilt, and for their return to the Land of Israel. With unbreakable faith, they continued to hold on to the vision given to them by the prophets of the wonderful culmination of history, a perfected world - living in peace.

Now, at long last, the first part of those heartfelt prayers have been miraculously answered, with Jews from all over the world coming home to the Promised Land, the Land of Israel; a nation not just surviving but thriving, as the astounded world looks on at what a wonder has arisen from the ashes.

For all the rest of the wonderful Hebrew prophecies of redemption to be fulfilled, it is essential that all of humanity now realize their higher G-d-given purpose, the creation of a kind and harmonious world, full of healthy, happy and caring people.

In order for such an elevation of human consciousness to occur, it is clear that our task must be to see to it that the illuminating wisdom of G-d's Torah becomes revealed to the whole world, thus bringing about the discovery of the hidden treasure that lies within all of us; the sublime perception of the inner light - the joy, beauty and wonder that is waiting to be experienced by our divine souls.

"When Isaiah tells us that 'the earth shall be filled with knowledge of G-d as water covers the sea' (Isaiah 11:9), what can this mean? The water and the sea are identical. It's like the English expression that we can't see the forest for the trees. One answer: When the Messiah comes, the world will be filled with such an awareness of G-d that we will finally realize that G-d and the world are one and the same. We will recognize that everything is G-d. The apocalyptic prophet Daniel echoes this verse of universal knowledge: 'Understanding shall be increased,' he says. Many things 'shall become clear and white... the wise shall understand' (Daniel 12:4,10). Things now opaque will become transparent. Things that now obscure our understanding will be cleared up. We will become enlightened."

RABBI ZALMAN SCHACHTER-SHALOMI

"Love is the only way to grasp another human being in the innermost core of his personality. No one can become fully aware of the very essence of another human being unless he loves him. By his love he is enabled to see the essential traits and features in the beloved person; and even more, he sees that which is potential in him, which is not yet actualized. Furthermore, by his love, the loving person enables the beloved person to actualize these potentialities. By making him aware of what he can be and of what he should become, he makes these potentialities come true."

VIKTOR FRANKL

"'You shall love your neighbor as yourself. *I am the Eternal G-d*' (Leviticus 19:18). Through the Bible, G-d has informed us that when you can truly love another, not for what you can get but rather for what you can give, then a third partner joins with you in that friendship, the King of kings. According to the Bible, G-d tells us that if you want to build a loving relationship with G-d, start by loving other members of humanity, all of whom are made in G-d's image."

GERALD SCHROEDER

The afterlife is seldom mentioned or alluded to in the Torah. This seems to suggest that G-d wants us to focus our attention on this life, here and now, where we may become aware of who we are and why we are here. We can then proceed to refine ourselves enough to discover that He has given us the opportunity of tasting heavenly joy right here on earth.

As G-d revealed to the Hebrew prophets, which they have passed on to us, He wants us to make every effort to transform this world into the wonderful place that He always intended it to be.

Evenso, life after the death of the body is indeed indicated to us in a number of places in the Torah, such as when we are not told that Enoch died, but rather that he 'walked with G-d' and then we are informed later in Genesis, with the passing of Abraham, Isaac and Jacob, that each of them were 'gathered unto their people.'

In I Samuel 28:3-19 we learn about Samuel's spirit rising from the grave and speaking to Saul. Then, we are given a vision in II Kings 2:11 of the departure of Elijah, reading that he 'went up to heaven in a whirlwind.'

Then, there is the faithful certainty expressed in Job 19:25-26, 'But as for me, I know that my Redeemer lives, and that He will witness at the last upon the dust; and when after my skin this is destroyed, then without my flesh shall I see G-d.'

The soul's journey beyond the body could very well be just what Shakespeare was hinting at when he made Hamlet tell Horatio that, 'There are more things in Heaven and Earth than are dreamt of in your philosophy…'

The View from Above

Rabbi Avraham Sutton writes: The following quotes are from an important document of our time written by Rachel Noam. On a cool but sunny Tel Aviv morning in January 1974, three months after the Yom Kippur war, Rachel had an out-of-the-body near-death experience (NDE) when she was struck by a 'heavy eighteen-foot wooden beam plunging from the scaffold atop a five-story structure.' Rachel was born and raised in Israel, and she wrote a book about her NDE, aptly entitled *The View from Above*:

"All at once, I felt I was outside my body, floating upward about twelve to fifteen feet above the sidewalk, watching the scene below. I did not know how I left my body or how I got up there. Everything happened so suddenly that I was caught completely by surprise. I saw a hefty woman bending over my body, trying to detect a sign of life in my motionless form…The woman, still kneeling beside me, looked up. 'Where's the building contractor!' she yelled…The other people joined in the shouting. On the roof, a young man emerged…I could see my body stretched out on the sidewalk. This is my body, I thought, but I am not inside it. I am looking at it from above. How is this possible? With what eyes am I seeing this, and where are my ears? How could I be hearing all this noise in the street?

It was strange to look at myself from the outside, knowing with certainty that this was my body. I was viewing it from a different perspective, since while I was inside my form I could not see it from outside. Now I was looking at my body the way I used to look at other people. I was baffled. Obviously, I existed, I was real, I was conscious, but not inside my frame. I always thought that 'I' and my body were identical. I did not know that I was a being that was more than just a physical body…

My sense of vision thus existed even without my physical eyes; the ability to reason existed outside my brain. All my life I had seen by means of my eyes, heard by means of my ears, reasoned by means of my brain. My consciousness had been fully integrated with my body into one inseparable unit. But now everything was different…I was surveying the scene from above, looking not only at other people but at myself, at my own material body.

A gradual change began to occur in my status of 'observer.' The events in the street began to fade away into darkness, and through this darkness I perceived a glimmer of brightness. As the radiance came closer it grew in intensity, becoming a glorious, powerful light, radiating an abundant flow of exalted spirituality. In harmony with this flow of illumination, the events in my life began to pass before my eyes. The images were three-dimensional, and I saw myself taking part in them. My entire life flashed by, from the day I was born until the very moment I fell to the ground.

The vision I saw was like a wide-screen film in which I had the starring role and was also the audience. The images streaked by very rapidly, yet not a single detail was omitted. It was like a video on which every incident is recorded, every musical note, every shade and color that enhanced my life, and now everything was being played back at high speed and with astounding sharpness. I do not remember the actual vision I saw. What endures in my memory is my surprise at the amazing vividness of the images, recalling long forgotten events and details. I wondered where this visual memory was coming from. How did I suddenly remember my entire infancy and childhood? These questions cropped up as I was watching the replay of my life. When the vision ended I asked myself whether it had really been my own life. I came to the conclusion that indeed it had been. The entire experience filled me with an indescribable sense of exalted happiness.

Once again, I saw the blinding luminescence, glowing in the soft velvety white, as if an infinite number of brightly flashing magic sparks were uniting in a burst of spectacular brilliance. I tried to compare this brilliant glow to the colors of light from various sources I had seen when I was inside my body, but even sunlight paled in comparison to this awesome superabundance of immeasurable brightness.

The magnificent stream of light was accompanied by a flow of sublime love, a kind of love I had never before experienced. It was unlike the love of parents toward their children, the love of friends and relatives or the love of Eretz Yisrael. Any love I had ever felt was nothing but a tiny speck compared to this exalted, powerful love...

Faced with this overpowering love, I felt incapable of remaining an independent entity; I simply melted away. I was too small to withstand the flow of goodness streaming toward me and into me. I tried to defend myself, to close my eyes, but I had no eyes to close! I had no way of hiding before the radiance. I had no body. I felt completely stripped of the outer shell that had protected me in this world. There was no possibility of evading the current of love that enwrapped me. No words can describe the enchantment, the wonder, the incomparable, infinite goodness...

I felt my very being dissolving. I knew that if I did not return to my body immediately it would be too late; my mortal being would cease to exist. I realized that the only reality was the reality of this light, the essence that prevails beyond the physical world...Any sense of independence, pride, anger, and desire vanished. All selfish tendencies disappeared, since my ego was about to be absorbed into the great light.

I felt a powerful bond with this marvelous presence. This was the will of a higher Power, a Being of infinite might. I felt a strong pull to become part of this wonderful eternal flow. It attracted me like a magnet with the power of its goodness, just as the earth exerts its attraction on the physical body. This magnetic force consisted of a confluence of goodness, light, faith, pleasure, self-effacement, joy, love, compassion, beauty, hope, and favor that drew me closer with its overwhelming magnetism.

Filled with awe and reverence I turned to the wonderful being and told Him about the extraordinary attraction He wielded over me. 'I am drawn to following my inclination,' I said, 'but I ask to be returned to my body. I ask to be given another opportunity in this world.' I went on to relate about Uzi (my husband), about the long time we had not seen each other because of the war, about our devotion to each other, about the meeting that was slated for this afternoon. I resisted the attraction of the higher will. I asked Him not to separate us. I told Him about my doubts and my search for the truth, until I had found Uzi and knew that he was truly meant for me, about my feeling that we were one, heart and soul…

My body and all I had done with it, that is to say, my life in the physical world, were described to me in the third person. There appeared before me a young woman who had lived her life the way she was brought up, and I—meaning my soul—was not this woman. I was not the body that had been living in this world. Never before did I feel like this. I always saw myself as one personality, a fusion of body and spirit. Only now did I realize that my body and I were two distinctly different entities that have united in this world for a certain purpose.

Looking at myself, I was overcome by a depressing thought. Too bad, I thought. She was so young and did not have a chance to live a meaningful life. The accident happened on my birthday. I was thinking about this young woman of twenty-two years of age whose lifeless body was lying on the street. I reviewed her/my life, a life without any real accomplishment. I felt as though I was waking up from a dream, the dream of my life. For the life I was living had flitted away; nothing was left of it. I sensed that I had not fulfilled my task in life. I knew that I had pursued false objectives. I understood that my soul had come down into my body to fulfill a certain assignment. I did not know what this assignment was, but I knew it had not been carried out. I was disappointed that the purpose of my life had not been accomplished.

The wondrous light did not interfere with my feelings and thoughts or influence them in any way. It was simply there; the absolute truth. It did not impose any demands on me, nor did it take responsibility regarding the purpose of my life. The light was simply present in my inner consciousness, an integral part of my feelings. It did not tell me the true meaning of life, what was its purpose or why I resided in my body all those years. It did not express any judgment regarding my actions of the past, whether they were good or bad. But simply by being there, surrounded by the light, I intuitively knew with absolute certainty that I had not fulfilled the mission for which I had been joined with my body in the corporeal world, in the *olam ha'asiyah*, the world of action.

I was overcome with a deep sense of regret for the time I had wasted... I was gripped by a powerful desire to come back and live a true life. I asked to return into my body that was sprawled on the street, to return to my loved ones, to life itself...I was filled with great compassion for my loved ones who would remain in this world, for my body, for the life I had wasted. A wave of pity swept over me.

I felt that this force of compassion brought me back into my body. Overcome with tenderness, with a boundless sense of compassion, I burst into tears. The hefty woman bent over me, and grabbing my hand, she coaxed me to get back on my feet. My soul returned to my body. I made it back. I do not know how I re-entered my body; everything happened so fast, and before I knew it, I had slipped back."

Rachel concludes:

"My body was shuddering with fright, shaken by the traumatic upheaval. It was only with great difficulty, and with overwhelming fear and convulsive spasms, that it managed to retain me within it...

My body was shaking with uncontrollable fits of sobbing, while I, still partially detached from my body, felt an ethereal happiness. I was fully conscious and completely aware of the condition of my body, as if I was still observing it from above, only this time I was inside my body...

I do not know how long I was outside my body. Perhaps it was only seconds, possibly minutes or more. Everything happened beyond the confines of time, transcending the limits of time. In the place where I was, time had no meaning; the concept of time did not apply. Down here, in the street, only a few seconds or minutes had elapsed, since by the time I returned to my body, people were still screaming for the contractor on the roof to come down".

Rachel goes on to describe how she was taken to the hospital, released, and finally arrived home late that afternoon. She cried for a long time, and yet she felt no pain. Before long, however, the pains did come, in the form of migraine headaches.

Rachel and her husband, Uzi Noam, had not been exposed to any real Judaic teachings. However, in the wake of her experience, they were both drawn to search for spirituality and were attracted to various forms of meditation. Nine years after her accident, on a fateful day in 1982, Rachel visited Esther, an old friend from her *kibbutz* who had married Yehudah:

"I arrived at their home [in Jerusalem] early in the evening. We were thrilled to see each other again. We talked about our lives…As we were talking, I noticed that Yehudah was wearing a small *yarmulka*. I expressed surprise. 'Well,' he replied forthrightly, 'I made up my mind to adopt a religious way of life.'

We sat around the kitchen table, had dinner, and talked late into the night. Yehudah and Esther were tired, and we decided to go to bed. I slept in the guest room on the second floor.

Before going upstairs, I noticed a book on the dining-room table. Since I am an avid reader, I decided to read a little before going to sleep. I took the book and went up to my room. I put my things in place, went to bed, and picked up the book. The title on the cover read, '*Siddur Tefillat Yesharim*—the Prayer of the Upright.' I started to read: '*Modeh ani lefanekha*—I gratefully thank You, *Melekh chai ve'kayam*—O living and eternal King, *Sh'hechezarta bi nishmati be'chemlah*—for having returned my soul within me with compassion; *rabbah emunatekha*—abundant is Your faithfulness.'

I was overwhelmed. I wanted to continue reading, and I realized at once that this book was unlike any other book I had ever read. This book I had to treat differently…Very slowly, the images I had seen during the accident began to reappear in my mind's eye, as though emerging from a haze. I continued reading: '*Elohai*—My Lord, *neshamah sh'natata bi*—the soul You placed within me *tehorah*—is pure. *Atah beratah*—You created it, *Atah yetzartah*—You formed it, *Atah nefachtah bi*—You breathed it into me. *Atah meshamerah bekirbi*—You safeguard it within me *veAtah atid litelah mimeni*—and eventually You will take it from me *ule'hachazirah bi*—and restore it to me *le'atid lavo*—in the future.'

14

My excitement soared. I had the urge to cry out, 'That's right. I know that this is true!' I wanted to tell people that I had personally experienced this. My soul was removed from my body, and it had been restored to it. But who would believe me? On the other hand, here it was, black on white, in the book that I had found on the dining room table, and obviously, people were reading it. What was going on here? Who had written this book? The questions kept coming in quick succession as I continued to read, 'As long as the soul is within me, I gratefully thank You, O God, my Lord, and the Lord of my forefathers, Master of all works, Lord of all souls. Blessed are You, O God, who restores souls to dead bodies.'

At this point my emotions peaked. Tears flowed freely down my cheeks. 'Lord of all souls who restores souls to dead bodies.' The thing I dared not speak about for so many years was written here plainly and lucidly. I was enthralled with the *siddur*. On and on I read without stopping, as if I were reading a suspenseful mystery novel. For about two hours, I read prayers and several chapters of *tehillim* (psalms). While reading, tears were streaming from my eyes. I wanted to scream, 'True. True. Whatever is written here is all true.'

I did not close my eyes all that night. Over and over, I browsed through the *siddur*, trying to digest in my mind what my eyes were reading. I realized that this was a book of commitment, of attachment to Hashem, and communicating with the *Shekhinah*; a book of supplications, assurances, and commandments. I did not understand the meaning of these commandments and how they were associated with the great light, but I felt intuitively that by dint of these commandments an abundant flow of goodness and kindness is drawn down from heaven to our world.

The tears that were flowing from my eyes reminded me of the uncontrollable crying spell I had after the accident. Once again, I was weeping irrepressibly, although by nature I am quite unemotional and unsentimental. In fact for many years I hardly cried at all. But these were tears of a different sort. I asked myself how it was possible that for thirty years I had not even once read the *siddur*.

That very night I decided to observe the *Shabbat*. I had no idea what *Shabbat* meant and what its observance entailed. The contrast between the socialist Saturday of the *kibbutz* and the *Shabbat kodesh* (holy

Sabbath) reflected in the *siddur* was as sharp as the disparity that separates darkness from light. I inferred from reading the *siddur* that *Shabbat* was a state of spiritual elevation, a condition I had never experienced.

This world is likened to darkness, the sages said. And waking up? Is it possible to wake up from the sleep of this world, 'to rise up in the middle of the night,' both literally and figuratively, 'in the midst of the night of this world?' Can we 'normal' people, in other words, transcend the existential condition in which we find ourselves, and see beyond the prism of our own consciousness, without having to die a clinical death?"

Isn't this what Adam-Chavah, Avraham-Sarah, Yitzchak-Rivkah, Yaacov-Rachel-Leah, Moshe-Tzipporah, David-Batsheva, and so many others did? And if they did it, and left us the map of their journey, is it then too audacious to want to follow in their footsteps? Especially at a time like this, in a generation such as ours, when this may not be considered a luxury but a duty?

The View from Above, published by Bristol, Rhein, and Englander, a subsidiary of C.I.S., Princeton, New Jersey, 1992; translated from the original Hebrew, *BaChazarah LeChayim—Return to Life*.

Excerpt from the talk by the Lubavitcher Rebbe of blessed memory on the Eve of Simchat Torah, 5746 (1985)

I should not complain if you were to translate Mashiach as the "redeemer – our righteous Mashiach," because in truth the *Nassi* of the generation is the redeemer of the generation.

The role of every generational Nassi and Shepherd of the Jewish People is to be the "Moshe Rabbeinu" of that generation.

As the Zohar teaches, "An emanation from Moshe is present in every generation. So much so, that every genuine Torah scholar is also a Moshe."

Inasmuch, as Moshe was the first redeemer and will also be the ultimate redeemer, it follows that the Moshe of every generation, the *Nassi* or leader, is also the Mashiach, the redeemer of that generation.

Consequently, when he appoints his envoys and they stand in his stead and carry out their mission with commitment, devotion and meticulous care, using their ten soul-powers, the envoy, the *"Shaliach"* (348) plus his ten soul-powers becomes *"Mashiach"* (358). In him the Sender – Mashiach – is revealed and then the ultimate revelation of Mashiach will actually come.

What Does Knowledge of G-d Mean?

The key to understanding the meaning of the 'knowledge of G-d' is to be found through pondering the statement written in the Torah that man has been created in G-d's image (Genesis 1:26).

Internalizing this knowledge, we can understand that just as G-d is kind, so in essence can we be kind, in the same way that G-d is just, so too can we be just, and in a similar manner, just as G-d loves us, so can we love each other.

Fulfilling our Divine mission to mirror the qualities of our Creator is solely dependent on our free will, because we are humans and not angels – because we are humans and not robots.

Our G-d-given role is to share our knowledge with all of humanity, spurred on by Isaiah's inspiring vision that informs us that the ultimate goal of mankind is to elevate human consciousness to the level that the world will be 'full of the knowledge of G-d, as the oceans cover the ocean bed' – a new world… of kindness, justice and love.

IN THE BEGINNING...
WAS THE BIG BANG

Let us start at the very beginning. The ancient Greeks believed that the universe had always existed, and until recently the idea that the universe had a beginning was an open question to scientists.

Since 1964, when Penzias and Wilson discovered the cosmic background radiation around 14 billion light years from Earth, proving that there is a limit to the expanding universe, it has been confirmed to the world of science that in the beginning there was a 'big bang' that started it all.

Now the question that needs to be answered is - how can the apparent creation of the universe 14 billion years ago be reconciled with the biblical account of the six days of Creation?

Gerald Schroeder gives an eye-opening explanation of this seeming dichotomy, demonstrating that in our post-Einsteinian world there is no contradiction here at all.

"How are we to stretch six days to encompass 14 billion years? Or the reverse, how do we squeeze 14 billion years into six days? The suggestion is not as absurd as it may first appear. In the Psalms of David we read, 'A thousand years are in Your eyes as a day that passes' (Psalms 90:4). This presents the possibility that G-d's perception of time is quite different from mankind's. But the literal meaning of this verse is qualitative. It has the feel of time seeming to pass at different rates for different participants in an event, but not necessarily being different in reality.

This verse in Psalms is reminiscent of the dilation of time dealt with in Einstein's revolutionary thought experiments. Einstein demonstrated that when a single event is viewed from two frames of reference, a thousand or even a billion years in one can indeed pass for days in the other.

The basis we seek for matching the biblical and cosmological calendars is, in fact, partly found in relativity. But Einstein's theory is no longer a theory. It is an empirically observed reality: Einstein's law of relativity tells us that dimensions in space and the passage of time are not absolute. Their measurement is an intimate function of the relationship between the observer and the observed. It seems incomprehensible that the flow of time, which is constant in our daily lives, can actually change – but it can.

During the development of our universe and prior to the appearance of mankind, G-d had not yet established a close relationship with the Earth. For from the first one or two days of the six days of Genesis, the Earth didn't even exist! Although Genesis 1:1 says 'In the beginning G-d created the heavens and the Earth,' the very next verse says that the Earth was void and unformed. The first verse of Genesis is a general statement meaning that, in the beginning, a primeval substance was created, and from this substance the heavens and the Earth would be made during the subsequent six days. This is explicitly stated later in Exodus 31:17: 'For six days G-d made the heavens and the Earth.' From what were the heavens and Earth 'made' during these six days? From the substance created 'in the beginning' of those six days. Because there was no Earth in the early universe, and no possibility of an intimate tie or a blending of the reference frames, there was no common calendar between G-d and the Earth.

According to Einstein's law of relativity, we now know it is impossible in an expanding universe to describe the elapsed time experienced during a sequence of events occurring in one part of the universe in a way that will be equal to the elapsed time for those same events when viewed from another part of the universe. The difference in motions and gravitational forces among the various galaxies, or even among the stars of a single galaxy, make the passage of time a very local affair. Time differs from place to place.

We can better understand this proven fact with the help of Einstein's thought experiment, in which the scientists aboard a speeding rocket and those in a stationary laboratory measured two very different times for a single event. This has no similarity to the claim by the late W.C. Fields that one night he spent a week in Philadelphia. His was an emotional sensation; ours is a physical fact. When we talk of a billion years, we don't mean it felt like a billion years. It was a billion years! If, during those first six days, a clock had been suspended in that part of the universe now occupied by the Earth, it would not necessarily have recorded 14 billion years. In the early universe, the curvature of space and time in this spot was probably very different from what it is now.

20

Instead, a compromise had to be made to describe the sequential development of the universe. This compromise was to choose, for the time preceding Adam, the Creator's own reference frame that viewed all the universe as a single entity.

Adam alone was given something new, unique in the universe – the living breath of G-d. It is only at the instant when G-d places in Adam this breath (in Hebrew, the *neshamah*), that both the created and Creator becomes inseparably linked. It is at this juncture that one out of billions of possible clocks was irrevocably chosen, by which all future acts would be measured."

Extracts from *Genesis and the Big Bang*

Schroeder goes on to describe the miracle of light becoming matter, and from that matter the emergence of organic life, living beings, and the culmination of G-d's creation, Adam – mankind:

"Light beams became alive, and became not only alive, but self-aware, and acquired the ability to wonder. The wonder is not whether genesis took six days or fourteen billion years or even eternity. The wonder is that it happened. Of that fact there is no debate in science. According to our best understanding of the universe and equally according to the most ancient commentaries on the book of Genesis, there was only one physical creation. Science refers to it as the big bang. The Bible calls it the creation of the heavens and the earth. Every physical object in this vast universe, including our human bodies, is built of the light of creation.

To elucidate the awesome and humbling implications of this incredible transition of light into life, consider the following better understood transition. In one hand I hold a clear glass jar containing the gas oxygen. In my other hand I hold a jar of hydrogen gas. I study the chemistry of these two gases and discover that, under the correct conditions, they can combine to make water, H_2O. Water neither looks nor acts like oxygen and hydrogen, but it is made up of them. When we drink water, we are drinking hydrogen and oxygen in a very special combination. In parallel, we humans and all the matter we see about us may not look like the condensed energy of the big-bang creation, but we are.

Concisely stated, the wisdom of G-d embedded in the energy of the big-bang creation laid the basis for that seemingly inert energy to metamorphose and become alive. And not merely alive, but even more than that – to become alive, and brimming with the sentient awareness of being alive. As Professor Wald stated so well: 'It is mind that has composed a physical universe that breeds life and so eventually evolves creatures that know and create: science-, art- and technology-making animals. In them the universe begins to know itself.'

Within every piece and aspect of the world, there lurks at its foundation the essence of wisdom, or mind, an emanation of the Force that brought it into being. As bizarre as it may seem, we will discover that the world in a very real sense, has a 'mind' of its own.

To understand how the dynamic Force manifests Itself in the ever changing world It created, we turn to the only two sources of relevant information: nature, that is, the world around us, and the Bible. The eighteenth-century theologian known as the Scholar, or Gaon, of Vilna taught that when the Torah was given on Sinai, it split into portions. Only one portion was retained in the written words of the Bible. The other portion was hidden in nature. And only when we finally discover that part of the Torah that was sequestered in nature will we be able to fully understand the word of G-d.

Psalms 19:1 declares: 'The heavens proclaim the glory of G-d; the sky declares His handiwork.' As a person who has worked in the sciences most of my life, in both physics and the earth and life sciences, I could not agree more fully. The hand of G-d reveals itself in the grandeur of galactic space as well as in the details of an atom. In both realms, vastly different in dimension, we can learn how G-d acts within this world It created. As nature provides the background for the biblical writings, so the Earth provides the substrate for the miracle of life."

Extracts from *G-d according to G-d*

Becoming aware of this miracle, and finding a way to achieve the raising of consciousness throughout the world, to allow all humanity to appreciate and celebrate all the wonders of G-d's creation, is described thus by Rabbi Zalman Shachter-Shalomi:

"The Baal Shem Tov used to say that the Master of the universe hid the spark of Messiah *bai dem gonif in peckel*, in the bag of the thief. The forces of evil in the universe, the Baal Shem taught, don't want the Mashiach to come, and put every kind of obstacle in the way. So the Master of the universe hides him where evil wouldn't think to look. Evil is still very much alive in the world today, whether in the torture chambers of despotic regimes, the rapacious behavior of our own corporations, domestic violence, or the neglect of millions of starving children. Our hopes can be so easily crushed. Yet in this very world is hope hidden, the Baal Shem Tov's simile insists, and in this very world we can find and nurture it.

'And G-d's spirit hovered on the face of the waters' (Genesis 1:2). This is the second verse of the creation story, describing the scene before creation began. The words *G-d's spirit,* a commentary says, are the name of Mashiach. 'And G-d's spirit' – the name of Mashiach – 'hovered on the face of the waters.' Have you ever seen a hen sitting on her eggs? Of course we can put them in a machine, an incubator, but that is not what is happening with mama hen. She sits on those eggs and says, 'Life…Life…Go into those chicks…' For days she sits there, sending that message down. That's the sense I get from the hovering of G-d's spirit in Genesis. The Hebrew word for 'hovers.' *merachefet,* is feminine. We feel the *Shekhinah,* the feminine face of G-d, brooding…broooooding over the waters to coax up life. One cell. More cells. We feel a constant sending down of revelation like a broody hen pushing down life, coaxing us into greater awareness, greater connectedness.

I believe the *Shekhinah* has been sending down that revelation from the first moment of creation. This is not the single overwhelming revelation of Torah from Sinai, whose echoes have ever since deteriorated with time. This is Torah that's coming to us right now. The seeds of this revelation are inside and all around us. Yes, our present world is flawed, but redemptive gems are hidden in its every corner, eluding all attempts to steal them away. We see a hint of this very different view of history and human potential contained in this quote from Talmud: 'Six thousand years the world will exist; two thousand chaos; two thousand Torah; two thousand the days of Messiah' (Avodah Zara 9a). This timeline imagines us ascending through ever higher levels of understanding. What we see here is not entropy but an evolution of consciousness, a continuing loosening up and releasing of revelation, a revelation we are accumulating day by day. Sinai pulls us back to the past, but Mashiach pulls us into the future. The mashiach seed in each of us dreams of a better future even while rooted in the imperfect present.

Our world is evolving toward a yet higher form of consciousness, a universal consciousness of the divine, a 'divinization' of the planet. How can we help to bring that transformation even while going on with our lives? In the Talmud there's a category of Jewish law known as *hilkheta le-mashichah,* halakhic rulings that demand too much of us in our current spiritual state but will take effect when the Mashiach comes. Rabbi Arthur Waskow asks; Why should we wait that long? Let us begin to live up to our highest aspirations Let's 'pre-tend,' in the sense of *tending* toward a goal before we achieve that, before we *are* that.

Judaism already has a sense of this. We call Shabbos *me-eyn olam ha-ba,* a taste of the world to come, and try to live that day as if Mashiach had already come. Reb Shmuel of Lubavitch wrote that every person should spend and experience at least fifteen minutes a day living like a *tzaddik gamur,* a complete tzaddik, a perfectly righteous person. In these brief periods spent in the presence of G-d, we can begin to capture a sense of not having to strive, of being there already."

Extracts from *Jewish with Feeling*

A LIGHT UNTO THE NATIONS

There is currently a surge in the publication of books that convey Torah teachings to the non-Jewish world, and such literature is being published at an ever-increasing rate for one good reason.

There is clearly a massive appetite and yearning among people of all nations, backgrounds and beliefs to understand what the Jews are really about, and to hear from them and understand what the Torah has to say about G-d's unfolding plan for the *Geulah* - the imminent redemption of the entire world.

This remarkable phenomenon of the awakening of so many holy souls among the nations to get closer to G-d and discover His Torah, is both mysterious and wonderful, and strongly suggests that their stirrings are directed from above, and are signs of the arrival of the *Geulah*.

When we take a look at Exodus 9:6, we see that the Children of Israel are to become a 'kingdom of priests and a holy nation' unto G-d. As the Jews' role is to act as G-d's faithful ambassadors to all of humanity, it follows that spreading Torah literature to the nations allows the Jewish people to bring G-d consciousness to all the inhabitants of the world, so as to transform mankind, and prepare us all for the promised *Geulah*.

Then, looking at G-d's words revealed to the prophet Isaiah in a Divine vision, we see Him talking about the (future) Temple in Jerusalem:

"I will bring them to My sacred mount, and let them rejoice in My house of prayer. Their burnt offerings and korbanot shall be welcome on My altar; for My House shall be called 'a house of prayer for all peoples'" *(Isaiah 56:7).*

How can all this possibly come to pass unless all the nations first get to know about this vision of our future given to us in G-d's Torah? The wide distribution of Torah literature will help facilitate this knowledge.

Because of the traditional Jewish teachings that, for very good reasons, it has been prohibited to reveal the deeper levels of Torah wisdom to non-Jews, this has hitherto inhibited and prevented the gentile world from discovering this beautiful and essential treasury of spiritual illumination.

In recognition that the world is ready, and the time has finally come, for the good of all people, to discard this taboo on making the Torah available to non-Jews, one of Israel's leading sages, Rabbi Yitzchak Ginsburgh, has laid great emphasis on the necessity of now spreading Torah teachings far and wide, calling this the fourth revolution in Torah learning:

THE FOURTH TORAH REVOLUTION

The First Torah Revolution

Some individuals have heard about the concept of the fourth revolution in Torah learning that we have been discussing for the past few years. Since it is the fourth in a series of changes that have altered the way in which Torah is learnt and by whom it is studied, we will first outline the three revolutions that preceded it. All four revolutions pertain to methods of teaching and studying Torah.

Together with the Torah that G-d gave Moses at Sinai, He gave 613 commandments to the Jewish People, and 7 commandments that must be observed by all mankind. The *Tanach* (the Hebrew Bible) comprises the Five Books of Moses (the Pentateuch), the Prophets, and the Writings. The *Tanach* is called the Written Torah. In addition to the Written Torah, G-d gave Moses the oral tradition, which explains how to correctly interpret the Written Torah according to the will of G-d (as mentioned in a previously given talk, the fact that G-d possesses will is a paradox). None of the commandments of the Torah can be fulfilled as G-d intended without the oral tradition. For reasons that are clear to G-d, the Giver of the Torah, the oral tradition was intended to remain oral, and G-d forbade it to be written down. It had to be passed on by word of mouth from generation to generation. This would enable the oral tradition to remain "organic," and grow and develop with a life of its own, without ever becoming static in book form.

About 2000 years after the giving of the Torah at Mt. Sinai, the oral tradition was still transmitted from generation to generation by word of mouth. However, it became clear to Rabbi Yehudah HaNassi (Rabbi Yehudah the Prince), the last sage of the era of the Tannaim—the Mishnaic era—that if they did not transcribe it now, the oral tradition would, G-d forbid, be forgotten. He saw that the generation was no longer capable of remembering the totality and the wholeness of the oral teachings. He instructed that the essence of the oral tradition, the Mishnah, be transcribed.

Although studying the Oral Law in book form had previously been prohibited, it now became permissible, and even a *mitzvah* to do so. The oral tradition underwent a total metamorphosis. Now we must write it down in order to convey it, so that it will never be forgotten.

The Second Torah Revolution

In Maimonides' times and for several generations following, it was forbidden for a sage to receive a financial stipend to study Torah. Every Jewish scholar worked for his living and studied Torah in his own time. He was not allowed to receive financial support from the community, nor to take charity to allow him to devote all his time and life to Torah study. A Torah scholar should be independent. Maimonides was so strict about this prohibition that he said that a Torah scholar who receives a stipend from the community in order to study, desecrates the Name of G-d. He offers examples of Talmudic sages, who toiled to make a living and studied Torah at their own expense. Maimonides states that combining work and studying sanctifies G-d's Name. This prohibition was still in force until about a thousand years ago, until the second Torah revolution took place. The reasoning was the same as with regard to the previous revolution. The rabbis were concerned that if they would continue this way, the Torah would be forgotten, G-d forbid.

Although it is good that a scholar is self-sufficient and does not rely on receiving charity from the community, the way life and society work are such that no-one can devote his entire life to Torah study without a source of livelihood. The sages of the generations after Maimonides, and most importantly Rabbi Yosef Karo (1488-1575), author of the *Shulchan Aruch* (Code of Jewish Law), authorized receiving a stipend from the community, to enable an individual to devote himself to Torah study, even as an a priori situation. Even today it is preferable for scholars to be self-dependent and to support themselves if they can. Nonetheless, anyone who cannot support himself and desires to devote himself to Torah study is permitted to accept support from the community; he is even instructed to do so.

The Third Torah Revolution

As we approach the coming of Mashiach, a positive feministic trend is manifesting in the Torah. As taught in Kabbalah, this trend is imperative to enable the redemption. Until about 150 years ago, there was no formal education for women in Jewish tradition. Women were educated at home. Like the original oral tradition, Jewish law and values were passed on from mother to daughter. There were no formal education systems for girls or women. Many girls were drawn to secular education and this led to them straying away from Jewish tradition. The great sages of the time instituted elementary education for girls, and even higher education. The Lubavitcher Rebbe explains that this is not only something that happened out of need, but it is because of a positive evolution in the essence of femininity.

Kabbalah teaches that in order for Mashiach to come, the stature of the male and the female must become equal. At a later stage, the feminine figure will rise even higher than the male. This manifests itself in reality as formal Torah education for women develops.

[Question: This sounds like modern feminism.] The feminist movement today around the world is indeed a secular movement. Nonetheless, any phenomenon that occurs in the world is an indication, a sign that a corresponding movement is happening inside. Secular feminism points to the fact that there is a corresponding rise of femininity taking place within the context of holiness. According to Kabbalah, the rise of the feminine figure is one of the indications that we are approaching the messianic era.

The Fourth Torah Revolution

As the Lubavitcher Rebbe taught, the way to usher in the era of Mashiach is to teach Torah and by doing so, to arouse Jewish sparks throughout the world to return to their source. Statistics state that in Catalonia, for example, one out of five people in the population is of Jewish ancestry. There are opinions that hold that the number of Marrano Jews in the world is between 100 and 500 million. In addition to those Jewish souls who were detached from their Judaism by force, there are also countless non-Jews who have an inner spark of Judaism that is waiting to be revitalized. Chassidut teaches that in order to hasten the redemption, these souls must become aware of this spark and unite with the Torah and the Jewish People. The Jewish People are the emissaries of G-d to bring the light of the Torah to the entire world.

A non-Jew who converts to Judaism is called "a convert who has converted." One of the great sages from almost a thousand years ago,

Rabbi Yehuda HaChassid (1150-1217), said this means that the convert was never a non-Jew. He was always potentially a convert, because from the moment he was born, he possessed a spark that was hidden. We cannot fathom why, but G-d, who is the ultimate paradox, knows the purpose behind everything. This is why at a certain point in the life of the convert, that spark becomes ignited. We do not know how many millions of such sparks exist around the world. Many people all over the world have become disillusioned with the traditions that they received, and they are spiritually open to seek the truth.

All over the world hearts are opening, and this is a trend that carries the message that Mashiach is coming. By spreading the light of the Torah, we can bring this trend to fruition. We cannot know who contains that potential spark. It might be everybody, or it might be a few people. Whichever the case, now is the time to ignite all the sparks around the world. The way to ignite the spark is by disseminating the light of the Torah, even the deepest Torah mysteries.

One of the most profound Torah mysteries is that the essence of G-d is paradoxical. We offered several examples of four different levels. Whenever we have four different levels of something, they correspond to the secret of the four letters of the essential Name of G-d, the Tetragrammaton (YKVK). Regarding faith in G-d, there are also four levels. Our purpose for initiating the fourth Torah revolution, spreading the light of the Torah to everyone, is to elevate everyone from his present level of faith to at least one level higher, if not to the highest of the four levels. So let us take a look at these levels of faith.

Four Levels of Faith – The World of Action – Idolatry

The lowest level of faith relates to *fear of punishment*, which can devolve into paganism, G-d forbid. We are commanded to believe that no force other than holiness controls us. Someone who sets his mind on evil is liable to become paranoid about things he thinks affect his life. As mentioned, the most basic teaching of the founder of Chassidut, the Baal Shem Tov, is not to fear anything in the world except for the one G-d, and to know that He is good. There is nothing else that can affect our lives. Wrongly placed fear is liable to degenerate into idolatry. This is the lowest level of faith, and it is not faith in G-d. This corresponds to the lowest of the four spiritual Worlds, *Assiyah* (the World of Action).

The essential statement of the Jewish belief system is, "Hear O Israel, *Havayah* is our G-d, G-d is One." The next three levels of faith correspond to three different interpretations of the Sages, regarding the meaning of "G-d is One."

The World of Formation – Negating Idolatry

The simplest interpretation is that there are no other gods except G-d; i.e., it negates idolatry. Not every form of idolatry involves worshipping physical idols. An idolater may believe that G-d created the world. He may believe that at one point, e.g., the Big Bang, a primal force brought the universe into being. This is the philosophical view that a first cause set the forces of nature (or other spiritual forces) into motion, but since then, it is no longer in conscious control of what is taking place. This philosophy is expressed in the phrase, "G-d has left the earth." G-d was the first cause, but He is no longer involved in what transpires in our world. Believing that reality is controlled by forces other than G-d, and worshipping them, or believing that everything that transpires is a chain of causes and effects is a form of sophisticated idolatry.

Denying such idolatry is our primary intention when we say that G-d is One. G-d is the primal cause, but He is as involved with creation in the present as He was at the outset. The belief system of *Yetzirah* (the World of Formation), the second highest spiritual World is denying that G-d, or some primal cause once put things into motion, but now He is no longer personally involved.

Although the belief system of *Yetzirah* admits that G-d is involved with the world, nonetheless, He might have partners. One example of this is belief in a "trinity." There is a controversy amongst the sages whether believing in such a religion is idolatry or not. Some hold the opinion that it is considered idolatry because it believes that there are other entities besides one G-d. Others state that it is not idolatry *per se* and for non-Jews it is permissible, because it only believes in partnership. According to this opinion, idolatry refers only to those who believe that G-d the Creator is no longer involved at all. Since that religion believes that G-d is still involved, even though He has two other gods working with Him, a non-Jew is permitted to believe in it, but for Jews it is forbidden. This opinion makes it clear that such a belief system is on a different level than idolatry.

One of Maimonides' outstanding innovations is that although they are not correct in their belief system, the "rebellious daughter religions" that were born out of Judaism represent a positive progression relative to the paganism that preceded them. Their establishment brings the world closer to the ultimate monotheistic belief in one G-d. The redemption depends on all mankind progressing towards a correct belief system. As mentioned, this relates to purifying one's thoughts of all diversions from belief in one G-d.

The World of Creation – Negating Partnership with G-d

Belief in G-d at the level of *Beri'ah* (the World of Creation) corresponds to the second interpretation of "G-d is One," i.e., that there are no other powers with free will who work in partnership with G-d.

Yet, even the oneness of G-d at this level does not relate to the G-d of Abraham, Isaac and Jacob in whom we believe. Of such a G-d, who is involved in the world and has no partners, we cannot yet say that His oneness is unique. We cannot yet say that "there is nothing like unto Him." As Maimonides teaches, there is something anthropomorphic about such a G-d. Maimonides is strongly opposed to anthropomorphism, because G-d is not like us, nor like anything else we can imagine. G-d has no comparison. The essence of such a belief system is that our logic is like G-d's logic.

The World of Emanation – Belief in G-d as the Bearer of Paradox

Unlike our logic, which is binary logic, G-d is paradoxical. Whereas in human logic, two opposites are contradictory, G-d is infinite, yet at the same time, He appears to us in finitude. In human logic, infinity and finitude are opposites and cannot exist simultaneously. Either something is finite or infinite, but it cannot be both at one and the same time. The true G-d of Abraham, Isaac, and Jacob contains any two apparent opposites simultaneously. This relates to the third interpretation of "G-d is One": "There is nothing like unto Him." As Maimonides states, the reality of G-d is the only true reality. We believe we are here, we are not dreaming, but we are not true reality. All our meditation and all the spiritual enlightenment that we will receive as we approach the messianic era, will deepen the revelation that G-d, the Creator, who is present here and now, so much so that I can speak to Him in prayer, is a personal G-d, not a philosophical G-d. Our G-d is not the impersonal G-d that Spinoza described and that Einstein believed in. G-d is a personal G-d. Nonetheless, He is simultaneously infinite. This is the paradox that only G-d can bear. Eastern religions solve the paradox by claiming that reality is a dream. They strive to abandon reality. For them there is also no purpose to life. They do not know the secret of true unity between infinite and finite. They cannot fathom how G-d has a passion to dwell in the lower, finite Worlds.

The goal of the fourth Torah revolution is to bring all of humanity to the level of *Atzilut* (the World of Emanation). This is the one true belief system: that G-d is absolutely unique. Even though one's goal in life is not to reach bliss (but to fulfill G-d's will), reaching the belief that G-d paradoxically is infinite yet takes an interest in every one of us is the ultimate bliss of life. This is the ultimate goodness and blessing of humanity.

Question: **Is meditation an acceptable tool for approaching G-d?**

Answer: Yes. According to some Torah opinions meditating is one of the 613 commandments. The purpose of meditation is to know G-d.

The Torah commands us, "You shall love G-d with all your heart and with all your soul and with all your might," but love is an emotion that happens naturally. How can one command someone to love? The Ba'al Shem Tov acknowledges that it is impossible to command someone to love someone or something. Nonetheless, you can command someone to meditate upon the positive qualities of the individual or object. Doing so will naturally arouse love. For example, a parent may tell their son, this girl is the best match for you. If the boy does not love the girl, but he thinks about all her positive qualities, it may ignite the potential for love (the same is true for a girl). Similarly, the commandment in the Torah to love G-d, means, "Contemplate those things about G-d that arouse your love." Moreover, by contemplating those things that arouse love with sincerity, even if you do not yet experience love in your heart, and even if it does not appear to work for you, at some level of your psyche you have fulfilled the commandment to love G-d.

Many souls around the world are attracted to the G-d of Israel. For a convert to convert he or she must be sincere. The most important example of an insincere conversion is when one converts to marry a Jewish man or woman. Nonetheless, if he/she converts and they do live a Jewish life, and fulfill the commandments, the conversion is valid. If they do not continue to live a Jewish life, the conversion is null and void.

In the past, anti-Semitism was so common that non-Jews were rarely attracted to the Jewish People. Even today, for every non-Jew who loves the Jewish People, there are far more individuals who hate the Jewish people. Nonetheless, because of our return to the land of Israel, and seeing our success in developing a government and an economy (despite all the spiritual issues that have yet to be resolved), many non-Jews are attracted to the Jewish faith.

Yet, falling in love with the Jewish People is not yet enough reason for conversion. If falling in love with one Jew, a Jewish boy or a Jewish girl is not sincere, then falling in love with the entire Jewish People is also not the ideal. We can only know that such a conversion is valid once the individual has converted and continues to live a Jewish life.

True conversion is falling in love with the G-d of Israel. Igniting the lost spark is falling in love with G-d, as Jacob fell in love with Rachel at first sight. When a convert recognizes G-d at first sight, he or she falls in love with G-d. Such a conversion is so potent that Maimonides says that the convert is greater than a Jew. Someone who recognizes G-d's unique Oneness and falls in love with Him and converts to Judaism is greater than someone who was born a Jew.

RABBI YITZCHAK GINSBURGH

PSALM 47

1. For the Conductor, a psalm by the sons of Korach.

2. All you nations, clap hands; sound [the shofar] to G-d with a sound of jubilation.

3. For the Eternal is most high, awesome; a great King over all the earth.

4. He subdues peoples under us, nations beneath our feet.

5. He chooses our heritage for us, the glory of Jacob whom He loves eternally.

6. G-d ascends through a blast, the Eternal through the sound of the shofar.

7. Sing, O sing to G-d; sing, O sing to our King.

8. For G-d is King over all the earth; sing, O man of understanding.

9. G-d reigns over the nations; G-d is seated on His holy throne.

10. The most noble of the nations are gathered, the nation of the G-d of Abraham; for the protectors of the earth belong to G-d; He is greatly exalted.

PSALM 57

1. For the Conductor, a plea to be spared destruction. By David, a michtam, when he fled from Saul in the cave.

2. Favor me, O G-d, favor me, for in You my soul took refuge, and in the shadow of Your wings I will take refuge until the disaster passes.

3. I will call to G-d the Most High; to the Almighty Who fulfills [His promise] to me.

4. He will send from heaven, and save me from the humiliation of those who long to swallow me, Selah; G-d will send forth His kindness and truth.

5. My soul is in the midst of lions, I lie among fiery men; their teeth are spears and arrows, their tongue a sharp sword.

6. Be exalted above the heavens, O G-d; let Your glory be upon all the earth.

7. They laid a trap for my steps, they bent down my soul; they dug a pit before me, [but] they themselves fell into it, Selah.

8. My heart is steadfast, O G-d, my heart is steadfast; I will sing and chant praise.

9. Awake, my soul! Awake, O harp and lyre! I shall awaken the dawn.

10. I will thank You among the nations, my Lord; I will praise You among the peoples.

11. For Your kindness reaches till the heavens, Your truth till the skies.

12. Be exalted above the heavens, O G-d; let Your glory be over all the earth.

PSALM 67

1. For the Conductor, a song with instrumental music, a psalm.

2. May G-d be gracious to us and bless us; may He make His countenance shine upon us forever,

3. that Your way be known on earth, Your salvation among all nations.

4. The nations will extol You, O G-d; all the nations will extol You.

5. The nations will rejoice and sing for joy, for You will judge the peoples justly and guide the nations on earth forever.

6. The peoples will extol You, O G-d; all the peoples will extol You,

7. for the earth will have yielded its produce, and G-d, our G-d, will bless us.

8. G-d will bless us; and all, from the farthest corners of the earth, shall fear Him.

PSALM 72

1. For Solomon. O G-d, impart Your justice to the king, and Your righteousness to the son of the king.

2. May he judge Your people with righteousness, Your poor with justice.

3. May the mountains bear peace to the nation, also the hills, in [reward for their] righteousness.

4. May he judge the nation's poor, save the children of the destitute, and crush the oppressor,

5. so that they will fear You as long as the sun [shines] and the moon endures, generation after generation.

6. May [his words] descend like rain upon cut grass, like raindrops that water the earth.

7. In his days may the righteous flourish, with much peace until the moon is no more.

8. And may he rule from sea to sea, and from the river until the ends of the earth.

9. May nobles kneel before him, and may his enemies lick the dust.

10. The kings of Tarshish and the islands will return tribute, the kings of Sheba and Seba will offer gifts.

11. All kings will bow to him, all nations will serve him;

12. for he rescues the needy one who cries out, the poor one who has no one to help him.

13. He pities the impoverished and needy, and saves the souls of the destitute.

14. He redeems their soul from deception and violence, and their blood is precious in his eyes.

15. He revives [the poor], and gives him of the gold of Sheba; and so [the poor] pray for him always, and bless him all day.

16. May there be abundant grain in the land, upon the mountaintops; may its fruit rustle like the [cedars of] Lebanon, and may [people] blossom from the city like the grass of the earth.

17. May his name endure forever; may his name be magnified as long as the sun [shines]. And all nations will bless themselves by him, they will praise him.

18. Blessed is the Eternal G-d, the G-d of Israel, Who alone performs wonders.

19. Blessed is His glorious Name forever, and may the whole earth be filled with His glory, Amen and Amen.

20. The prayers of David, son of Jesse, are concluded

PSALM 77

1. For the Conductor, on the yedutun, by Asaph, a psalm.

2. [I raise] my voice to G-d and cry out; [I raise] my voice to G-d and He will listen to me.

3. On the day of my distress I sought my Lord. My wound oozes at night and does not abate; my soul refuses to be consoled.

4. I remember G-d and I moan; I speak and my spirit faints, Selah.

5. You grasped my eyelids; I am broken, I cannot speak.

6. I think of olden days, of ancient years.

7. During the night I recall my music, I meditate with my heart, and my spirit searches:

8. Is it for eternity that my Lord forsakes [me], nevermore to be appeased?

9. Has His kindness ceased forever? Has He sealed the decree for all generations?

10. Has G-d forgotten mercy? Has He in anger restrained His compassion forever?

11. I said, "It is to terrify me that the right hand of the Most High changes."

12. I remember the deeds of Yah, when I remember Your wonders of long ago.

13. I meditate on all Your works, and speak of Your deeds.

14. O G-d, Your way is in sanctity; what G-d is as great as G-d?

15. You are the G-d Who works wonders; You make Your might known among the nations.

16. You redeemed Your people with a mighty arm, the children of Jacob and Joseph, Selah.

17. The waters saw You, O G-d, the waters saw You and trembled; even the deep shuddered.

18. The clouds streamed water, the heavens sounded forth, even Your arrows flew about.

19. The sound of Your thunder was in the rolling wind; lightning lit up the world; the earth trembled and quaked.

20. Your way was through the sea, Your path through the mighty waters; and Your footsteps were not known.

21. You led Your people like a flock, by the hand of Moses and Aaron

PSALM 99

1. When the Eternal will reveal His kingship, the nations will tremble; the earth will quake before Him Who is enthroned upon the cherubim,

2. [before] the Eternal Who is in Zion, Who is great and exalted above all the peoples.

3. They will extol Your Name which is great, awesome and holy.

4. And [they will praise] the might of the King Who loves justice. You have established uprightness; You have made [the laws of] justice and righteousness in Jacob.

5. Exalt the Eternal our G-d, and bow down at His footstool; He is holy.

6. Moses and Aaron among His priests, and Samuel among those who invoke His Name, would call upon the Lord and He would answer them.

7. He would speak to them from a pillar of cloud; they observed His testimonies and the decrees which He gave them.

8. Eternal our G-d, You have answered them; You were a forgiving G-d for their sake, yet bringing retribution for their own misdeeds.

9. Exalt the Lord our G-d, and bow down at His holy mountain, for the Eternal our G-d is holy.

PSALM 117

1. Praise the Eternal, all you nations; extol Him, all you peoples.

2. For His kindness was mighty over us, and the truth of the Eternal is everlasting. Halleluyah!

PSALM 138

1. By David. I will thank You with all my heart, in the presence of princes I shall praise You.

2. I will bow toward Your Holy Sanctuary, and praise Your Name for Your kindness and for Your truth; for You have exalted Your word above all Your Names.

3. On the day that I called out You answered me, You emboldened me, [You put] strength in my soul.

4. O Eternal, all the kings of the land will give thanks to You when they hear the words of Your mouth.

5. And they will sing of the Eternal's ways, for the glory of the Lord is great.

6. For though the Eternal is exalted, He sees the lowly; the High One castigates from afar.

7. If I walk in the midst of distress, keep me alive; against the wrath of my enemies stretch out Your hand, and let Your right hand deliver me.

8. The Eternal will achieve on my behalf; O Eternal, Your kindness is forever, do not forsake the work of Your hands.

PSALM 145

1. A psalm of praise by David: I will exalt You, my G-d the King, and bless Your Name forever.

2. Every day I will bless You, and extol Your Name forever.

3. The Eternal is great and exceedingly exalted; there is no limit to His greatness.

4. One generation to another will laud Your works, and tell of Your mighty acts.

5. I will speak of the splendor of Your glorious majesty and of Your wondrous deeds.

6. They will proclaim the might of Your awesome acts, and I will recount Your greatness.

7. They will express the remembrance of Your abounding goodness, and sing of Your righteousness.

8. The Eternal is gracious and compassionate, slow to anger and of great kindness.

9. The Eternal is good to all, and His mercies extend over all His works.

10. O Eternal, all Your works will give thanks to You, and Your pious ones will bless You.

11. They will declare the glory of Your kingdom, and tell of Your strength,

12. to make known to men His mighty acts, and the glorious majesty of His kingdom.

13. Your kingship is a kingship over all worlds, and Your dominion is throughout all generations.

14. The Lord supports all who fall, and straightens all who are bent.

15. The eyes of all look expectantly to You, and You give them their food at the proper time.

16. You open Your hand and satisfy the desire of every living thing.

17. The Eternal is righteous in all His ways, and benevolent in all His deeds

18. The Lord is close to all who call upon Him, to all who call upon Him in truth.

19. He fulfills the desire of those who fear Him, hears their cry and delivers them.

20. The Eternal watches over all who love Him, and will destroy all the wicked.

21. My mouth will utter the praise of the Lord, and let all flesh bless His holy Name forever.

PSALM 150

1. Halleluyah! Praise G-d in His holiness; praise Him in the firmament of His strength.

2. Praise Him for His mighty acts; praise Him according to His abundant greatness.

3. Praise Him with the call of the shofar; praise Him with harp and lyre.

4. Praise Him with timbrel and dance; praise Him with stringed instruments and flute.

5. Praise Him with resounding cymbals; praise Him with clanging cymbals.

6. Let everything that has breath praise G-d. Halleluyah!

FAITH – EMUNAH

"When a person understands that everything that happens to them is for their own good, this is a glimpse of the World to Come."

(*Likutey Moharan* I:4)

Rebbe Nachman's teachings on how to have faith (emunah) that G-d loves us, and everything He does is entirely for our benefit is beautifully described by Avraham Greenbaum writing in *Garden of the Souls*:

"In his story of "The Sophisticate and the Simpleton", Rebbe Nachman tells how the Sophisticate proves to his own satisfaction that there is no King over the world. Afire with the zeal of the self-righteous, the Sophisticate sets off with a companion on a world-wide mission to try to persuade everyone else of this "truth". They lose everything they have, but still the Sophisticate refuses to admit he might be wrong.

Finally, the Devil sends for them. The Sophisticate ridicules the idea of the Devil - he no more believes in evil than in good. But to back down from accepting the Devil's dare would mean an unacceptable loss of face. So the Sophisticate has to go off with his companion together with the Devil's messenger.

Rebbe Nachman relates: "The Devil captured the Sophisticate and his companion, and brought them to a quicksand bog. The Devil sat on a throne in the middle of this bog, and he threw the Sophisticate and his companion into the mud. The bog was thick and sticky like glue, and they could not move at all in it.

"When the Devil and his cohorts began to torture these two sophisticates, they screamed out, `Fiends! Why are you torturing us? Does such a thing as the Devil really exist? You are fiends, and you are torturing us for nothing.' These two sophisticates still did not believe in the Devil. They thought these were wicked people, who were torturing them for no reason..." (Rabbi Nachman's Stories p.193)

The Sophisticate had made it his life's purpose to deny G-d. He is the exemplar of skepticism, the opposite of faith. In place of the King he has put himself on the throne. Spurning external authority and tradition, he is going to be the arbiter of what exists. The Sophisticate will believe nothing unless he can see it with his own eyes or understand it with human reason. For him, there is only one world, the one he can look at, touch and feel, the world of nature. He will not admit that levels of spiritual mystery might exist that could be invisible to him.

A world with no King is a world without order - a world of chance, with no such thing as absolute good and evil, no reward for righteousness and punishment for sin. And thus when suffering comes to the Sophisticate, he can find no meaning in it. Having thrown away the idea of Divine Justice, he cannot relate his suffering to what he has done. He cannot learn or grow from it. Being unable to explain it, he finds it pointlessly cruel. And because the Sophisticate has turned his back on G-d, G-d turns His back on him, as it were, hiding His unity, punishing him through a devilish plurality of bizarre, meaningless forces: "You are fiends, and you are torturing us for nothing!"

It is his own self that is blinding the Sophisticate to the truth. This is why he has to be punished for so long. Only when he is totally battered down and crushed will he be forced to admit defeat - to admit that there is a power greater than himself. At the end of the story, when he sees he is unable to help himself, the Sophisticate finally realizes that only through the intervention of a saintly Miracle Worker could he be saved. "...And he was forced to admit to the truth, that there is a King" (ibid. p.195).

The quicksand bog - what a graphic metaphor for some of the things people go through in this world! How many times in life do we find ourselves stuck: no matter which way we try, twist and turn, we are just caught in thick mud, unable to get free.

And how do we respond? Well we're only human. A Sophisticate nags away in the heart: "Why? Why? ... This is not fair! ... What did I do to deserve this? ... Why do You do this to me? If this is what You do, why should I believe in You? Why should I keep to Your rules?"

How much of life goes on anger, complaints, protests, rancour, recriminations, bitterness, hatred. How much energy gets spent on vain struggles against windmills, endless campaigns against the apparent perpetrators of the wrongs and injustices people feel they have suffered. "Fiends, you are torturing us for nothing!"

"Everything G-d does is for the best"

At the other end of the spectrum is Rabbi Akiva, exemplar of faith. The Talmud relates how once Rabbi Akiva went on a journey. He came to a town and asked if anyone could put him up for the night. The inhospitable inhabitants all refused. Still, Rabbi Akiva said, *Kol de-avid Rachmana, le-tov avid* - "Everything G-d does is for the best," and he went and spent the night in the field. With him he had a lamp, a rooster to wake him and a donkey to ride on. But a wind came and blew out the light, a cat came and ate his rooster, and a lion came and ate the donkey. Rabbi Akiva was left all alone in the dark, but he still said, "Everything G-d does is for the best."

In the middle of the night a band of marauders came, sacked the town and took all the inhabitants captive. Then Rabbi Akiva said, "Now I see how everything the Holy One does is for the best. If my lamp had been alight, they would have seen me. If the rooster had crowed and the donkey had brayed, they would have known where I was and taken me as well" (*Berachot* 60b).

A story not about suffering, perhaps - at least, as far as Rabbi Akiva is concerned - but certainly one about things not going as planned. Yet Rabbi Akiva is a believer. Not just intellectually. His belief has a practical effect on the way he conducts his life and responds to what happens to him. He has the humility to accept that a force higher than himself controls the world in general and his life in particular. Belief does not mean that Rabbi Akiva succumbs to passivity and resignation. No, he is a doer - he has lots of plans and he tries doing whatever he can. But when things don't go the way he thought they should, he doesn't get annoyed. He puts up with a bit of inconvenience - because he believes G-d knows better than he does how to run things.

Rabbi Akiva calls G-d *Rachmana* - the Loving One. No matter what happens, the Loving One is working everything out for the best, even when Rabbi Akiva can least see how. And in the end it was indeed revealed how the hand of Providence had been working at every stage to do what was necessary to save the Tzaddik from the punishment of the wicked.

The Talmud tells us Rabbi Akiva spent the night "in the field". Perhaps the Supernal Field, the Garden of the Souls Rebbe Nachman speaks of in his lesson - the ultimate, joyous goal of all of life. Closing his eyes to the hardships of the physical world, Rabbi Akiva takes himself off to the "field": he focusses his inner eye on the spiritual world of Unity.

Rabbi Akiva was a living expression of Emunah, our faith in the One G-d as we express it every day in the Shema: Hear, Israel, HaShem, Our G-d, HaShem is One. G-d in Himself is beyond any comprehension. He reveals Himself to the world through different facets. There are the aspects of Chesed, Mercy, alluded to in the name HaShem (YKVK), and Gevurah, Might, Strict Judgement, alluded to in the name Elokim. In the Shema we assert that the two facets are one: HaShem is Elokim. Elokim is HaShem. HaShem is One.

Life has different sides. Sometimes things smile at us and we see the Mercy. Other times we feel under a cloud, nothing goes the way we want it, things seem bad. But in the Shema we express our faith that One G-d is in control of all the different sides of life. Even the hard things in life are from G-d. When things go differently from the way we might want, it doesn't mean that life is cruel without purpose. Hardship and suffering are not arbitrary. They come from G-d as much as the good things.

G-d is Rachmana, the Loving One. Everything He does to us is for our ultimate good. G-d is perfection, and the greatest love is that we should come close to Him and know Him. But we are like growing children who still want to be little: we don't like leaving behind our childhood indulgences - materialism - for the sake of maturity - the life of the spirit. The worldly ego says "I want things my way". But good parents know that if you love your child you have to be firm. You have to deny the child things that will be bad in the long run, and you have to push the child to make an effort to attain the things that will be good.

The hand of Strict Judgement operates in unity with the side of Tender Mercy. Both complement each other, working towards the same goal - the bestowal of G-d's love on us, which means the revelation of Himself. G-d is One - *EChaD*. The sum of the numerical values of these letters - the gematria - is 13. This is the same as the gematria of *AHaVaH* - Love. Thirteen attributes of Lovingkindness. Perfect unity.

When we say the Shema, the declaration of our faith, we put our hand over our eyes and close them tight. This material world was set up to challenge us. Things cannot be taken at face value here - appearances can be very deceptive. G-d is often so hidden, especially when things are bad, and we cannot see where any of it is leading. We close our eyes tight and cover them over with our hand, so as to focus the inner eye on the world of truth. Shema Yisrael, HaShem is Elokim. Elokim is HaShem. Mercy involves Firmness. Firmness is a part of Mercy. HaShem is One.

Why do people suffer?

All this is very fine as long as things are going reasonably well, and the level of suffering is tolerable. A single night without lights, alarm clock, or transportation may be bearable. In Rabbi Akiva's case the meaning of the mysterious happenings of the night was revealed the very next morning. But how many things in this world work out with a happy ending so quickly?

People go through protracted periods of acute suffering, physical and mental. There are so many different kinds of suffering - *lo aleinu* - please, please, not on us! There are all kinds of illnesses, terrible accidents, tragic losses, catastrophic reverses, the shattering of hopes and dreams, whether in families, relationships, careers, businesses. There is the suffering that comes directly from HaShem, and the suffering that is channeled through the agency of others - criminals, persecutors, and even unwitting innocents. We go through suffering ourselves, we see those around us, our loved ones, going through it. And too often we see no happy ending at all in this world - only tragedy, loss, heartache and grief.

Physical pain can sometimes be eased. There may be a cure, or at least the agony can be lessened with pain-killers. But what about the anguish of the soul? So many of the things people go through seem so incomprehensible. It might be easier to accept if we could see something that made clear sense in terms of human logic: suffering as the punishment for evil, the wicked suffer, the good do not. Things are nothing like so simple. Suffering afflicts not only the wicked, but good, upright, hard-working citizens, and even the greatest Tzaddikim. What did the six million victims of the Holocaust do - men, women, children, babies in arms? We are not atheists. We want to believe. But how? How can we begin to understand any of this, let alone accept it?

Silence... and an echo of a voice

At the end of his life, Rabbi Akiva himself suffered the most terrible martyrdom. He was flayed alive at the hands of the Roman oppressors. Rabbi Akiva was undoubtedly a Tzaddik Gamur, a Perfect Tzaddik: a saint, a towering scholar of the Holy Torah, an outstanding leader of his people. He has to go through such suffering? Suffering that baffles his students, that baffles Moshe Rabbeinu, that baffles the very angels...?

Yet at the climax of his ordeal, Rabbi Akiva is saying "Shema Yisrael". Wracked with pain, face to face with the most horrible death, Rabbi Akiva asserts the unity of G-d. Even in his pain and torment he sees the hand of G-d. How?

There is no answer.

And there is an answer.

And both are correct.

The Talmud (*Menachot* 29b) depicts Moshe ascending on high and seeing the soul of Rabbi Akiva, who was to plumb greater depths in Moshe's Torah than even Moshe himself. "Show me his reward!" asks Moshe - and he is shown a vision of Rabbi Akiva being flayed alive with iron combs. "Is this the reward for Torah?" asks Moshe. And G-d replies, "Be silent! This is the way it arose in the Divine thought." Be silent. It is part of the Divine plan. How? Why? No answer. Only silence. Everything is cloaked in mystery.

But the Talmud gives us another dimension of Rabbi Akiva's martyrdom. In Berachot 61b we are told how when Rabbi Akiva was taken out to be killed, it was time for saying "Shema". Rabbi Akiva was taking on himself the kingship of Heaven. His students ask him "Rabbeinu, this too?" And Rabbi Akiva answers: "All my days I've been troubled about this verse - `love G-d... with all your soul'- which means `even if He takes your soul'. I said, When will I have the opportunity to fulfill it? Now that the moment has come, shall I not fulfill it?" Rabbi Akiva drew out the word Echad ... until his soul went out on Echad.

The Talmud continues: The Ministering Angels asked G-d, "Is this the reward for Torah?" Exactly the same question as Moshe's. Only this time there is an answer. Moshe Rabbeinu was flesh and blood - a man living in this world, where life ends with death, and beyond death nothing is visible. But the angels are pure spirit, they are not subject to death, and can therefore understand something which mortal man, this side of death, cannot.

To the angels G-d gave an answer: "Their portion is life..." And a Bat Kol - the "Echo of a Voice" - the distant voice of prophetic intuition - came forth, spelling out the answer for those willing to hear it: "Happy are you, Rabbi Akiva, for you are called to the life of the World to Come!" Such martyrs and sufferers may suffer in this world, but ultimately they inherit life, the true life of the World to Come. Eternal life.

For Moshe, in this world, there was no answer - because in terms of this world alone there can be no answer. If we look at suffering only in the perspective of this visible, temporary world, it must remain incomprehensible. If our only criteria of success and happiness are those of this world - material wealth and pleasures - how can we possibly come to terms with sickness, pain, loss, destruction...? Too often the older people get the more they seem under attack - lonely, bereft of their dear ones, incapacitated, ever more helpless, riddled with aches, pains, chronic disease. Is this where life leads to and nothing more?

The answer is that the purpose lies beyond this world, in a realm we cannot see with our physical eyes - a realm only the angels can begin to "see". The most that can be revealed in this world is through a Bat Kol - a faint echo of a voice - the voice of Torah wisdom - for those willing to hear it. It is a matter of belief. It has to be, because this side of death we cannot see what lies beyond. Here we cannot see that for the soul there is no death, only eternal life.

Belief in the World to Come is the foundation of Torah teaching about the meaning of suffering - and indeed of all the different things people go through in this world. This world is the ante-chamber, the place of preparation, leading to the World to Come. Only when we understand that the soul is living and enduring, that its sojourn in a transitory body in a transitory world is a preparation for something higher, can we begin to make sense of the things people go through in this world.

"He's laughing!"

A funeral procession was passing in front of Rebbe Nachman's window. The people in the procession were crying and wailing. But the Rebbe commented, "Presumably the dead man is laughing in his heart at the way they're crying over him. When someone dies, people cry over him as if to say: How good if you had lived in this world even longer and suffered even more trials and torments, and then you would have had even more bitterness... At least this will be the end of his pain and suffering, because once he has gone through anything he might have to go through [in Gehenom] he will enjoy the reward for his good deeds in this world" (Tzaddik #446.).

So the World to Come is the place of laughter and joy - does that mean we have to wait till then to be happy? Are we supposed to just grit our teeth and bear the pains of this world in the meantime? Could that be the message of Rebbe Nachman of Breslov - who taught the world to rejoice, that "It's a great mitzvah to be happy all the time" - ?

Well, what is the happiness Rebbe Nachman is teaching us? Much of the world is obsessed with a hell-bent pursuit of the blithe, breezy light-headedness that advertisements, films, romances and the like parade as happiness. But even if it exists, it is only a fool's paradise, good as long as reality can be held at bay. This has nothing to do with the holy joy and happiness - the Simchah - that Rebbe Nachman is teaching us. The power and depth of true Simchah is that it is founded on facing reality, not evading it.

We are not supposed to wait for the next world until we can be happy. There is a way to find joy even amidst the suffering of this world - through belief in the World to Come. The stronger our belief in it, and the more we work for it and look forward to it, the more we can accept and rejoice in the trials of this world - because we believe, we know, that their ultimate purpose is good. We discover the real good that is in this world. This is the essence of Rebbe Nachman's message to us in "Garden of the Souls".

"For the ultimate goal is completely good, and in the end everything will turn out to have been for good. Even when bad things happen and you are beset with troubles and suffering, G-d forbid, if you will look at the ultimate purpose, you will see these things are not bad at all, they are actually a very great favor. All suffering is sent from G-d intentionally for your own ultimate good. It could be to remind you to return to G-d, or to cleanse and scour you of your sins. If so, suffering is really very beneficial. G-d's intention is certainly only for good.

"Whatever evil and suffering you go through, G-d forbid, if you will just look at the ultimate goal - G-d's purpose - you will not experience it as suffering at all. On the contrary, you will be filled with joy at so much good when you look at the purpose of this suffering. Because the ultimate purpose is entirely good, all unity. And the deep truth is, there is no evil at all in the world: everything is good.

"Then why do we feel pain when we suffer? The pain people go through because of their suffering is only because their Da'at - divine understanding - is taken from them, and they are unable to focus on the ultimate purpose, which is entirely good. It is then that they feel the pain and sorrow of their suffering. But when understanding is present and one keeps one's attention on the ultimate goal, one does not feel pain and suffering at all" (*Likutey Moharan* I:65,3).

What is Da'at? "*VeyaDA'ta* - Know today and take it to your heart that HaShem is Elokim - in heaven above and on the earth below - there is none other" (Deuteronomy 4:39). Know: HaShem is Elokim. The two facets of life - Chesed, Mercy, and Gevurah, Might and Strict Judgement - are one. HaShem is Elokim. Elokim is HaShem. HaShem is One. It's a matter of faith. The faith of Rabbi Akiva. When problems came up, he said "Everything the Loving One does is for the best". And at the moment of excruciating pain and torment, he closed his eyes completely to this world in a supreme effort to focus only on the truth beyond it: "Shema Yisrael, HaShem Elokeinu, HaShem Echad".

The Rabbis (*Pesachim* 50a) asked about the prophecy "On that day HaShem will be one and His name one" (Zechariah 14:9). "Why 'on *that* day'? Isn't G-d one today?" And they answered that today, for good things we bless G-d as "good and beneficent", while for bad things we bless Him as "true Judge". In other words, in this world, we do instinctively distinguish between the different facets of life, between good and bad. The underlying unity is for the most part concealed. But in future, said the Rabbis - "on that day" - we will bless G-d for everything as "good and beneficent"! In the future, in the World to Come, even G-d's severity will be revealed as an aspect of His love. Everything will be seen to be a single unity.

Da'at means taking the longer perspective - understanding the real place of this world and the things that happen in it in the total scheme of things. Thus when we relate the bad things that happen to our ultimate purpose, when we believe determinedly that they are for our good, we can get a glimpse even here and now of the inexpressible joy of the World to Come. This is the meaning of Rebbe Nachman's saying: "When a person understands that everything that happens to them is for their own good, this is a glimpse of the World to Come - *Me-eyn Olam Ha-ba*" (*Likutey Moharan* I:4).

Olam Ha-ba itself is beyond this world - "No eye has seen it" (Isaiah 64:3) - because it cannot be seen with the physical eye. We have to close our physical eyes to the outward appearance of this world, and focus our thoughts on the ultimate purpose - Unity. Then we can have me-eyn Olam Ha-ba - a fleeting glimpse, an indescribable taste! The word me-eyn literally means "from the eye" - signifying the appearance of something. We can have a fleeting glimpse of the way things "look" in the future world. And the hint as to how is: me-eyn, "from the eye". Where are our eyes? How do we look at things?

"I never had a bad day in my whole life"

After all the teachings and explanations about the way we are supposed to respond to the hard knocks and blows of life, the practical question still remains: How? How do you look on the good side when the pain hurts? "When a person understands that everything that happens is for their own good..." Is it possible to understand this at the moment of actual suffering, when the ultimate purpose is far beyond our range of vision?

Let's not even talk about trying to achieve the high level of having clear knowledge that things are all for the good. Say we just want to believe it even without being able to see it. It's one thing to believe in theory. How do we get the belief into our hearts and respond accordingly? It may be a lot to expect to experience joy at the height of pain, but let's talk about less intense suffering. In more normal circumstances, when things go against us in the way they do one way or another practically every day of our lives, how can we learn to accept the superiority of the Divine wisdom with love? How can we remain cheerful and happy instead of kicking, screaming and complaining? How, in this benighted world, can we learn to look at the things we don't like differently?

A man once came with these very same questions to Rabbi Dov Ber, the Maggid of Mezeritch: "How can I learn to accept the bad things in life?" And the Maggid said to him: "I have a disciple who will be able to help you. His name is Reb Zusya. He lives in such and such a place. Go to him."

The man found a low, broken-down house betraying all the signs of extreme poverty and suffering. When Reb Zusya appeared, the man explained why he had come. "But I don't understand," said Reb Zusya. "Why did the Maggid send you to me? I never had a bad day in my whole life!"

A famous Chassidic tale... but did the Reb Zusya of the story really exist? Was the actual Reb Zusya of Anipoli really like that? Could someone in real life live in abject poverty with all that it entails - hunger, deprivation, discomfort, sickness, pain - and be in Gan Eden? Didn't Reb Zusya feel the discomfort - when so many people in their luxury villas and mansions, with more food, clothes and money than they themselves could ever need, are mournful, depressed and full of complaints?

Perhaps some of us look at Reb Zusya and say in our hearts, he probably wasn't used to anything better. I could never accept anything like that in my life. Is there an element of pride in such a reaction? How demeaning to have to go through that. And fear? Please, G-d, don't ever do that to me! Maybe we have a sneaking suspicion that learning to look at things differently doesn't really make the pain go away! And in a childish way, isn't that what we really want - that pain and suffering should just disappear? Is Reb Zusya's way of looking at things really a solution?

We may certainly admire Reb Zusya and wonder at his greatness. But what does his example do for us? Is such a level practically possible for you and me? How can ordinary people with all their human frailties, needs, desires, standards, etc. possibly experience pain, hardship and adversity as being good?

Perhaps the man who came to the Maggid with his questions felt exactly the same way, as he stood there contemplating Reb Zusya. Why did the Maggid send me here? What kind of an answer is this supposed to be? Yet the question remains. How do we cope with suffering? Because it is with us whether we like it or not.

Self-Centered or G-d-Centered

You might have thought the Maggid should have responded by sending the man home with some kind of practical self-improvement program to deepen his faith. How was he supposed to benefit from going to see Reb Zusya?

Well, first let's consider what Reb Zusya really was. He was a living example of bittul - one of the key concepts in "Garden of the Souls". The root idea of bittul is to make something into nothing, to nullify or cancel. In the terminology of Mussar and Chassidut, bittul refers to a state of self-surrender and transcendence. One recognizes oneself as a creation of G-d, dependent on G-d, a servant of G-d. Bittul is the opposite of yeshut, most ordinary people's regular state, in which they experience themselves as separate and independent entities, with an outlook and responses that are basically ego-centered.

Pure bittul is not a state that can be experienced permanently in this life. Even to talk about bittul as an experience is somewhat of a contradiction in terms, because "experience" implies that there is someone having the experience, whereas in bittul one is taken quite out of oneself. Rebbe Nachman makes it clear in "Garden of the Souls" (and see *Likutey Moharan* I:4,9) that even the most advanced spiritual seekers go into bittul only for fleeting moments - at the height of intense prayer and meditation, for example.

Yet there is a more everyday aspect of bittul that everyone is capable of achieving. Step by step, one works towards a fundamental shift of orientation in which self-centeredness is sacrificed for G-d-centeredness. One learns to accept that G-d's goals for our lives, as taught in the Torah, are more vitally important than the mundane goals and projects dear to our material egos. G-d's guidelines about how to make a success of life are truer and more firmly founded than any of the ideas we or those around us could ever think up by ourselves.

Why do we not experience G-d's goodness at all times if not because our whole attention is focussed on what we want and desire, our own goals, projects and purposes. We want to control things and have them go our way. We get tense, anxious, and fearful that things won't go the way we want. And when they finally don't, we are frustrated, angry, outraged, depressed...

Where are our eyes? Rebbe Nachman teaches: The sun shines constantly, it's just that you can't always see the light because the earth is in the way - even though the earth is very small in comparison with the sun. The "sun" is G-dly light - the light of the Torah and the Tzaddikim. The "earth" is earthly materialism - This World, with all its desires and obsessions.

Says Rebbe Nachman: You may be standing facing a great mountain, but if you take even a little coin and hold it in front of your eyes, you won't be able to see the mountain. So it is when we come into this world: we get sunk amidst the vanities of this world and think there's nothing better - because this tiny little world prevents us from seeing the great light of the Torah, which is so many thousands of times greater. The world is there in front of our eyes and stops us from seeing any further. If only we could remove the barriers from in front of our eyes. If only we could lift our heads up a bit and look a little further. We would see such a wonderful light - the light of the Torah and the Tzaddikim - and we would not feel we were missing anything.

"Oy va-voy!" cried the Baal Shem Tov, "The world is full of such incredible radiance, such wonderful secrets... And there's a little hand stuck in front of the eyes, stopping them seeing these great lights" (*Likutey Moharan* I:133).

If we could just lift up our heads a bit and look a little further. Bittul in the practical sense means just this - lifting ourselves up so as to see beyond our ego-bound interests and ideas. Little by little one learns to erase the part which says "I want things this way. I can only accept things as good if they come out my way." And thus one comes to accept that "You decreed it that way, and You really do know better."

Reb Zusya had achieved this bittul to perfection. That is how he could accept that everything is from G-d and therefore good. "I never had a bad day in my whole life."

A Chip at the Ego

Emunah - faith - is the answer, and Emunah means taking a different perspective. This may help explain why the Maggid didn't just send his questioner home to work on his faith by himself. He had to come out of his ego-bound self. That's why he had to go to see a Tzaddik - someone who could take him out, and show him a whole other perspective on life. The first step towards Emunah is one of self-deflation. We have to acknowledge that we ourselves do not have all the right answers. We do not know. We are not perfect. There are others who are far wiser and saintlier.

The Tzaddik is a kind of spiritual mirror you go to in order to see yourself by comparison and understand where you're really holding (*Likutey Moharan* I:19,2). This is why Rebbe Nachman's lesson to us in "Garden of the Souls" begins with the idea of leadership. The souls in the Garden cannot grow without the Master of the Field. Only with outside guidance can we rise above ourselves and come to a higher perspective.

The road to bittul can be long and arduous. Really trying to put the Tzaddik's teachings into practice may involve extensive re-evaluation of one's goals and priorities, many doubts and questions, difficult adjustments to habitual patterns and lifestyle, trying new ways, facing challenges, falling down, trying to pick oneself up and start again.

Do the perspectives of Rabbi Akiva or Reb Zusya seem impossibly hard to achieve? That should not deter us from making a start. It was Reb Zusya himself who taught us to be ourselves and start from where we are. "At the Heavenly judgement, I won't be afraid if they ask me why I wasn't like Abraham, Isaac and Jacob. When they ask me, Why weren't you like Reb Zusya - that's when I'll be afraid!"

And who am I? Am I so wise that I know what is really best for me - best in this world and best in terms of my ultimate destiny? Is the way I think things ought to be necessarily the way they should be? Am I entitled to expect that everything should always go exactly the way I want? Have I done right all my life - am I so pure and saintly that nothing needs fixing in my life. Do I understand what needs fixing and how? And when I know things need fixing, do I do everything necessary of my own accord, without needing any kind of push or nudge from the outside?

And for all that, "...Your kindnesses are never exhausted... and Your tender mercies are never ended!"

Who understands the meaning of the suffering in this world - lo aleinu - please, please, not on us! Who knows who suffers and how? Who understands the pain in another person's heart? Who understands the pain in our own hearts? But there is one kind of suffering we can perhaps do something about: the suffering caused by the Sophisticate in us.

The Sophisticate had dethroned the King and made himself king. That was why he was made to suffer - until his pride was broken down and he finally had to admit: I am not the king. G-d is the King."

In poverty, ill health or disability, we can still thank G-d for all His abundant goodness and gifts to us.

Whatever the mistakes of the past, we can put them behind us, and overcome any anxiety and depression that we may feel, by holding onto our faith.

We are exactly where we are meant to be, and we can all be grateful for even one's present circumstances, because they are precisely what we need at this time, and where we are is just the right place for now, and good for us, because G-d, our Creator loves each one of us, and is kind and forgiving.

Speaking of faith, in his work *Tanya*, Rabbi Shneur Zalman of Liadi writes: "The essential thing is the (mental) training to habituate one's mind and thought continuously, that it ever remain fixed in his heart and mind, that everything one sees with one's eyes - the heavens and earth, and all that is therein – constitutes the outer garments of the King, the Holy One, blessed be He. In this way he will be constantly aware of their inwardness and vitality. This is also implicit in the word **Emunah** (faith), which is a term indicating 'training', to which a man habituates himself, like a craftsman who trains his hands…"

As Rabbi Shalom Arush says: "All of life's questions have one universal answer – **Emunah**. Emunah is like a master key to life's locked dilemmas.

Emunah is the original biblical Hebrew term for a firm belief in a single, supreme, omniscient, benevolent, spiritual, supernatural, and all-powerful Creator of the universe, which we refer to as G-d (or **HaShem**, which means 'the name', so that we don't risk using G-d's name in vain). He alone cares for each of us in a unique, tailor-made fashion according to our own individual needs.

Everything that happens to us in life is the product of HaShem's will and personal intervention in our lives, which we refer to as Divine

Providence. Divine Providence is designed to help us perform our task in life.

Divine Providence not only determines events on a global scale, it dictates the tiniest details in the universe, such as the evening meal of a worm. Our lives in their entirety – HaShem's Divine Providence-oriented decisions. HaShem decides when we succeed and when we fail, when times are easy and when they're hard.

According to the Kabbalah, or esoteric thought, completing one's soul correction, or **tikkun,** is the loftiest achievement a person can accomplish in this material world. Oftentimes, we must suffer or experience hardship in order to attain a higher spiritual level or correction of the soul, just like a champion athlete must withstand excruciating training sessions to reach higher achievements and peak performance.

Once we develop a deep sense of Emunah that HaShem, by way of Divine Providence, does everything for our ultimate benefit to guide us on the path of our needed soul correction, the puzzle-pieces of life suddenly come together in a picture of striking clarity. With these principles in mind, Emunah becomes the universal answer to all of life's questions."

Even when things appear to get very trying, if we can only learn how to recognize that this is all for our benefit, we will see our difficulties as a G-d-given opportunity for us to grow.

Rebbe Nachman explains this in the following way: "Every person must constantly advance from level to level. When the time comes for someone to advance from one level to the next, he must first experience a fall before he can rise up. The whole purpose of the fall is to prepare for the advance. So no matter how far you might fall, you should never allow yourself to be discouraged. Remain firm and resolute. In the end, the fall will be transformed into a great advance. This is its whole purpose. People think this only applies to those on very high levels who are continually advancing from level to level. But it also holds true even for people on the lowest of levels. For G-d is good to all."

While acknowledging that in real life, understanding this is easier said than done, Rabbi Jacob Immanuel Schochet describes how having faith and trust in G-d will lead to joyfulness:

"He who believes in G-d whole-heartedly, of necessity also trusts in Him with a powerful *bitachon* (trust), a *bitachon* that assures that one will not be afraid of anything. This *bitachon* means total peace of mind from all and anything that might cause anxiety; for there is an absorbing reliance on the One in whom we trust to be an impenetrable shield of protection against all and any harm. In turn, *bitachon* and *emunah* must lead to *simchah* (joy). For the servant who trusts in his master, and who truly believes that his service is meaningful and effective, will serve with joy."

JOY

'It is a great mitzvah to be happy at all times'

(*Likutey Moharan ii, 24*)

'A joyful heart is good medicine…'

(Proverbs 17:22)

PSALM 1

1. Happy is the man that has not walked in the counsel of the wicked, nor stood in the path of sinners, nor sat in the company of scoffers.

2. Rather, his desire is in the Torah of the Eternal, and in His Torah he meditates day and night.

3. He shall be like a tree planted by streams of water, that yields its fruit in its season, and whose leaf does not wither; and all that he does shall prosper.

4. Not so the wicked; rather, they are like the chaff that the wind drives away.

5. Therefore the wicked will not endure in judgement, nor sinners in the assembly of the righteous.

6. For the Eternal minds the way of the righteous, but the way of the wicked will perish.

PSALM 16

1. A michtam, by David. Watch over me, O G-d, for I have put my trust in You.

2. You, [my soul,] have said to G-d, "You are my Lord; You are not obligated to benefit me."

3. For the sake of the holy ones who lie in the earth, and for the mighty-all my desires are fulfilled in their merit.

4. Those who hasten after other [gods], their sorrows shall increase; I will not offer their libations of blood, nor take their names upon my lips.

5. The Eternal is my allotted portion and my share; You guide my destiny.

6. Portions have fallen to me in pleasant places; indeed, a beautiful inheritance is mine.

7. I bless the Eternal Who has advised me; even in the nights my intellect admonishes me.

8. I have set the Eternal before me at all times; because He is at my right hand, I shall not falter.

9. Therefore my heart rejoices and my soul exults; my flesh, too, rests secure.

10. For You will not abandon my soul to the oblivion, nor will You allow Your pious one to see ruination.

11. Make known to me the path of life, that I may be satiated with the joy of Your presence, with the bliss of Your right hand forever.

PSALM 32

1. By David, a maskil. Fortunate is he whose transgression is forgiven, whose sin is covered.

2. Fortunate is the man to whom the Eternal does not reckon his sin, and in whose spirit there is no deceit.

3. When I was silent, my limbs wore away through my wailing all day long.

4. For day and night Your hand was heavy upon me; my marrow became [dry] as the droughts of summer, Selah.

5. My sin I made known to You, my iniquity I did not cover. I said, "I will confess my transgressions to the Eternal," and You have forgiven the iniquity of my transgression forever.

6. For this let every pious man pray to You, at a time when You may be found; indeed, the flood of many waters will not reach him.

7. You are a refuge to me; protect me from distress; surround me with songs of deliverance forever.

8. I will enlighten you and educate you in the path you should go; I will advise you with what I have seen.

9. Be not like a horse, like a mule, senseless, that must be muzzled with bit and bridle when being adorned, so that it not come near you.

10. Many are the agonies of the wicked, but he who trusts in the Eternal is surrounded by kindness.

11. Rejoice in the Eternal and exult, you righteous ones! Sing joyously, all you upright of heart!

PSALM 97

1. When the Eternal will reveal His kingship, the earth will exult; the multitudes of islands will rejoice.

2. Clouds and dense darkness will surround Him; justice and mercy will be the foundation of His throne.

3. Fire will go before Him and consume His foes all around.

4. His lightnings will illuminate the world; the earth will see and tremble.

5. The mountains will melt like wax before the Eternal, before the Master of all the earth.

6. The heavens will declare His justice, and all the nations will behold His glory.

7. All who worship graven images, who take pride in idols, will be ashamed; all idol worshippers will prostrate themselves before Him.

8. Zion will hear and rejoice, the towns of Judah will exult, because of Your judgments, O Eternal.

9. For You, Eternal, transcend all the earth; You are exceedingly exalted above all the supernal beings.

10. You who love the Eternal, hate evil; He watches over the souls of His pious ones, He saves them from the hand of the wicked.

11. Light is sown for the righteous, and joy for the upright in heart.

12. Rejoice in the Eternal, you righteous, and extol His holy Name.

PSALM 100

1. A psalm of thanksgiving. Let all the earth sing in jubilation to the Eternal.

2. Serve the Eternal with joy; come before Him with exultation.

3. Know that the Eternal is G-d; He has made us and we are His, His people and the sheep of His pasture.

4. Enter His gates with gratitude, His courtyards with praise; give thanks to Him, bless His Name.

5. For the Eternal is good; His kindness is everlasting, and His faithfulness is for all generations.

* * *

Speaking of joy, Rabbi Avraham Greenbaum writes, "Rebbe Nachman of Breslov repeatedly emphasized the importance of being happy:

"Azamra − *'I will sing!'* - is his teaching about the way to happiness, by always seeking out the good points in ourselves and others."

* * *

Make every effort to maintain a happy, positive outlook at all times. It is a natural human tendency to become discouraged and depressed because of the hardships of life: everyone has their full share of suffering. That is why you must force yourself to be happy at all times. Use every possible way to bring yourself to joy, even by joking or acting a little crazy!

(Likutey Moharan II, 24)

* * *

If you are happy, the whole world benefits.

(Netiv Tzaddik 71)

* * *

A happy front

Even if you are upset and unhappy, you can at least put on a happy front. At first you may not feel genuinely happy in your heart. Even so, if you *act* happy you will eventually attain true happiness and joy.

(Sichot Haran #74)

Good humor

Having a sense of humor is good on three conditions:
1) You do not insult others. 2) You are not vulgar. 3) You do not present yourself in a good light to the detriment of others.

(Siach Sarfey Kodesh 1-13)

* * *

Finding the good points

You must search for the good in yourself.

When you start looking deep within yourself, you may think there is no good in you at all. You may feel you are full of evil: a negative voice inside you may try to drive you into depression. But you must not allow yourself to fall into depression. Search until you find some little good in you. For how could it be that you never did anything good in your whole life?

When you start to examine the good you have done, you may see many flaws. Maybe you did what you did for the wrong reasons and with the wrong attitude. Even so, how could it be that your mitzvah or good deed contains no good at all? It *must* contain some element of good.

69

You must search and search until you find some good point within you to give you new life and happiness. When you discover the good that is still inside you, you literally swing the scales from guilt to merit. This will enable you to return to G-d. The good you find inside you will give you new life and bring joy to your soul.

Having found one good point, you must continue searching until you find another. Even if you think this good point is also full of flaws, you must still search for some good in it. In the same way, you must continue finding more and more good points.

This is how songs are made! In essence, music is made by sifting the good from the bad. The musician has to find the "good spirit" – the good air – and reject the bad. A musical instrument is a vessel containing air. The musician produces the sounds by causing the air to vibrate. His task is to move his hands on the instrument in such a way as to produce good spirit, "good vibrations", while avoiding the "bad vibrations" – the dissonant winds of gloom and depression.

When a person refuses to allow himself to fall into despair but instead vitalizes himself by seeking out and gathering together his positive points, this produces melodies, and he can then pray, sing and give thanks to G-d.

When a person recognizes the wrong he has done and how grossly materialistic and impure he is, he can become so depressed that he is completely incapable of praying. He simply cannot open his mouth to G-d. This is because of the deep sorrow and heaviness that overcome him when he sees his overwhelming distance from G-d.

But finding your good points can give you new life. Even if you know you have done wrong and caused damage and that you are far from G-d, you must search until you find the good that is still inside you. This will give you new life and make you truly happy. You are certainly entitled to feel the greatest joy over every good point you find in yourself, because each good point comes from the holy soul within you. The new life and joy you will gain from this path will enable you to pray, sing and give thanks to G-d.

(Likutey Moharan I, 282)

True humility

A person should never let his own smallness insignificance and humility cover up his true greatness. For sometimes a person downgrades himself to excess and forgets that he still has many amazing attributes.

(Siach Sarfey Kodesh 1-34)

* * *

A settled mind

The main reason why people are far from G-d is because their minds are not settled and they do not pause to consider the purpose of their existence. But when a person is happy, his mind becomes settled and he is able to understand things clearly.

Someone who is anxious and depressed finds it impossible to direct his thoughts where he wants. It is hard for him to calm and settle his mind. Only when a person is happy can he direct his thoughts wherever he wants and settle his mind.

Joy is the world of freedom - "for you shall go out with *joy*" (Isaiah 55:12). Through joy we become free and leave our exile. When a person maintains a happy, joyous attitude, his mind and thoughts become free and he is no longer in exile. He can then direct his thoughts as he wants and settle his mind so as to focus on his goal and draw close to G-d.

(Likutey Moharan II, 10)

* * *

Join the dance

Sometimes a group of people happily dancing together take hold of someone who is standing miserable and depressed on the outside. They pull him into the dance circle despite himself, forcing him to rejoice with them.

Similarly, when a person is happy, his pain and sadness may move to the sidelines. But a higher level is to pursue the sadness itself and "pull it into the dance circle," turning it into joy.

If you truly set your mind to it, you will find that even amidst your worst troubles and suffering there is always a way you can turn all your sadness into joy. True joy is when you forcibly transform your very sadness and depression into happiness.

(Likutey Moharan II, 23)

* * *

The difference between brokenheartedness and depression

Having a broken heart and being depressed are two quite different things.

Depression is rooted in the unholy "other side" and G-d hates it. But being brokenhearted and contrite over one's sins and shortcomings is very dear and precious to G-d.

It would be very good to be brokenhearted all day. But this could easily throw most people into gloom and depression. You should therefore set aside some time each day for heartbreak. Seclude yourself with G-d for a given time and break your heart with regret over your sins. Then be happy for the rest of the day.

(Sichot Haran #41)

Being gloomy and depressed is like being angry with G-d for not satisfying one's desires. But someone with a broken heart is like a small child pleading with his father or crying out and complaining to him for being distant.

(Sichot Haran #42)

* * *

After heartbreak comes joy. Being happy later on is a true sign of having a broken heart.

(Sichot Haran #45)

* * *

Hold onto the good times

You should always try to be happy and serve G-d with joy, and even if you sometimes fall short of your level, you can still encourage yourself by thinking of earlier times when you did have a taste of the light.

A number of blind people can all take hold of one sighted person and follow him trustingly. A blind man trusts his stick and follows it even though he sees nothing. How much more should you follow your own self - because the light did shine on you previously, arousing and inspiring you to serve G-d.

Maybe you feel you have fallen and that your eyes and heart are closed. Even so, you should still hold onto those earlier days. Just as you were aroused and encouraged to serve G-d then, strengthen yourself now by following the sense of arousal you felt then. G-d will soon help you and His light will shine on you again.

(Likutey Moharan I, 222)

The Pursuit of Joy by Rabbi Jonathan Sacks

"Happiness, said Aristotle, is the ultimate goal at which all humans aim. But in Judaism it is not necessarily so. Happiness is a high value. Ashrei, the closest Hebrew word to happiness, is the first word of the book of Psalms. We say the prayer known as Ashrei three times each day. We can surely endorse the phrase in the American Declaration of Independence that among the inalienable rights of humankind are life, liberty and the pursuit of happiness.

But Ashrei is not the central value of the Hebrew Bible. Occurring almost ten times as frequently is the word simchah, joy. It is one of the fundamental themes of Deuteronomy as a book. The root s-m-ch appears only once in each of Genesis, Exodus, Leviticus and Numbers, but no less than twelve times in Deuteronomy. It lies at the heart of the Mosaic vision of life in the Land of Israel. That is where we serve G-d with joy.

Joy plays a key role in two contexts in this week's parsha (Ki Tavo). One has to do with the bringing of first-fruits to the Temple in Jerusalem. After describing the ceremony that took place, the Torah concludes: "Then you will rejoice in all the good things that the Lord your G-d has given you and your family, along with the Levites and the stranger in your midst" (Deuteronomy 26:11).

The other context is quite different and astonishing. It occurs in the context of the curses. There are two passages of curses in the Torah, one in Leviticus 26, the other in Deuteronomy 28. The differences are notable. The curses in Leviticus end on a note of hope. Those in Deuteronomy end in bleak despair. The Leviticus curses speak of a total abandonment of Judaism by the people. The people walk be-keri with G-d, variously translated as 'with hostility,' 'rebelliously,' or 'contemptuously.' But the curses in Deuteronomy are provoked simply "because you did not serve the Lord your G-d with joy and gladness of heart out of the abundance of all things" (28:47).

Now, joylessness may not be the best way to live, but it is surely not even a sin, let alone one that warrants a litany of curses. What does the Torah mean when it attributes national disaster to a lack of joy? Why does joy seem to matter in Judaism more than happiness? To answer these questions we have first to understand the difference between happiness and joy. This is how the first Psalm describes the happy life:

Happy is the man who has not walked in the counsel of the wicked, nor stood in the way of sinners or sat where scoffers sit. But his desire is in the Torah of the Lord; on his Torah he meditates day and night. He shall be like a tree planted by streams of water, bearing its fruit in its season, and its leaf does not wither; and in all that he does he prospers (Psalms 1:1-3).

This is a serene and blessed life, granted to one who lives in accordance with the Torah. Like a tree, such a life has roots. It is not blown this way and that by every passing wind or whim. Such people bear fruit, stay firm, survive and thrive. Yet for all that, happiness is the state of mind of an individual.

Simchah in the Torah is never about individuals. It is always about something we share. A newly married man does not serve in the army for a year, says the Torah, so that he can stay at home "and bring joy to the wife he has married" (Deut. 24:5). You shall bring all your offerings to the central sanctuary, says Moses, so that "There, in the presence of the Lord your G-d, you and your families shall eat and rejoice in all you have put your hand to, because the Lord your G-d has blessed you." (Deut. 12:7). The festivals as described in Deuteronomy are days of joy, precisely because they are occasions of collective celebration: "you, your sons and daughters, your male and female servants, the Levites in your towns, and the strangers, the fatherless and the widows living among you" (16:11). Simchah is joy shared. It is not something we experience in solitude.

Happiness is an attitude to life as a whole, while joy lives in the moment. As J. D. Salinger once said: "Happiness is a solid, joy is a liquid." Happiness is something you pursue. But joy is not. It discovers you. It has to do with a sense of connection to other people or to G-d. It comes from a different realm than happiness. It is a social emotion. It is the exhilaration we feel when we merge with others. It is the redemption of solitude.

Paradoxically, the biblical book most focused on joy is precisely the one often thought of as the unhappiest of all, Kohelet, a.k.a. Ecclesiastes. Kohelet is notoriously the man who had everything, yet describes it all as hevel, a word he uses almost forty times in the space of the book, and variously translated as 'meaningless, pointless, futile, empty,' or as the King James Bible famously rendered it, 'vanity.' In fact, though, Kohelet uses the word simchah seventeen times, that is, more than the whole of the Mosaic books together. After every one of his meditations on the pointlessness of life, Kohelet ends with an exhortation to joy:

I know that there is nothing better for people than to rejoice and do good while they live (3:12).

So I saw that there is nothing better for a person than to rejoice in his work, because that is his lot (3:22).

So I commend rejoicing in life, because there is nothing better for a person under the sun than to eat and drink and rejoice (8:15).

However many years anyone may live, let him rejoice in them all (11:8).

My argument is that Kohelet can only be understood if we realise that hevel does not mean 'pointless, empty, or futile.' It means 'a shallow breath.' Kohelet is a meditation on mortality. However long we live, we know we will one day die. Our lives are a mere microsecond in the history of the universe. The cosmos lasts forever while we, living, breathing mortals, are a mere fleeting breath.

Kohelet is obsessed by this because it threatens to rob life of any certainty. We will never live to see the long-term results of our endeavours. Moses did not lead the people into the Promised Land. His sons did not follow him to greatness. Even he, the greatest of prophets, could not foresee that he would be remembered for all time as the greatest leader the Jewish people ever had. In contrast, Van Gogh sold only one painting in his lifetime. He could not have known that he would eventually be hailed as one of the greatest painters of modern times. We do not know what our heirs will do with what we leave them. We cannot know how, or if, we will be remembered. How then are we to find meaning in life?

Kohelet eventually finds it not in happiness but in joy – because joy lives not in thoughts of tomorrow, but in the grateful acceptance and celebration of today. We are here; we are alive; we are among others who share our sense of jubilation. We are living in G-d's land, enjoying His blessing, eating the produce of His earth, watered by His rain, brought to fruition under His sun, breathing the air He breathed into us, living the life He renews in us each day. And yes, we do not know what tomorrow may bring; and yes, we are surrounded by enemies; and yes, it was never the safe or easy option to be a Jew. But when we focus on the moment, allowing ourselves to dance, sing and give thanks, when we do things for their own sake not for any other reward, when we let go of our separateness and become a voice in the holy city's choir, then there is joy.

Kierkegaard once wrote: "It takes moral courage to grieve; it takes religious courage to rejoice." It is one of the most poignant facts about Judaism and the Jewish people that our history has been shot through with tragedy, yet Jews never lost the capacity to rejoice, to celebrate in the heart of darkness, to sing the Lord's song even in a strange land. There are eastern faiths that promise peace of mind if we can train ourselves into habits of acceptance. Epicurus taught his disciples to avoid risks like marriage or a career in public life. Neither of these approaches is to be negated, yet Judaism is not a religion of acceptance, nor have Jews tended to seek the risk-free life. We can survive the failures and defeats if we never lose the capacity for joy. On Sukkot, we leave the security and comfort of our houses and live in a shack exposed to the wind, the cold and the rain. Yet we call it z'man simchateinu, our season of joy. That is no small part of what it is to be a Jew.

Hence Moses' insistence that the capacity for joy is what gives the Jewish people the strength to endure. Without it, we become vulnerable to the multiple disasters set out in the curses in Deuteronomy. Celebrating together binds us as a people: that and the gratitude and humility that come from seeing our achievements not as self-made but as the blessings of G-d. The pursuit of happiness can lead, ultimately, to self-regard and indifference to the sufferings of others. It can lead to risk-averse behaviour and a failure to 'dare greatly.' Not so, joy. Joy connects us to others and to G-d. Joy is the ability to celebrate life as such, knowing that whatever tomorrow may bring, we are here today, under G-d's heaven, in the universe He made, to which He has invited us as His guests.

Toward the end of his life, having been deaf for twenty years, Beethoven composed one of the greatest pieces of music ever written, his Ninth Symphony. Intuitively he sensed that this work needed the sound of human voices. It became the West's first choral symphony. The words he set to music were Schiller's Ode to Joy. I think of Judaism as an ode to joy. Like Beethoven, Jews have known suffering, isolation, hardship and rejection, yet they never lacked the religious courage to rejoice. A people that can know insecurity and still feel joy is one that can never be defeated, for its spirit can never be broken nor its hope destroyed."

"Happiness is a skill that can be learned. The essential factor whether or not you will live a happy life is not based so much on external factors such as wealth, success, or fame, but on your attitudes towards life, towards yourself, towards other people, and towards events and situations. Regardless of how you have viewed those areas in the past, you can presently change your attitudes and master the attribute of happiness.

"Western society has been influenced by a number of harmful myths concerning happiness and emotions. Anyone exposed to those ideas is likely to suffer needlessly. One of the most pernicious ideas prevalent today is that happiness is dependent on external events and situations, and that a person has limited control over his general emotional state. The Torah point of view is that happiness is possible for everyone and is an obligation. A person's thinking plays a major role in his emotions. We have great potential to think in a manner conducive to happiness. While a growing number of schools of thought subscribe to this view (e.g. cognitive therapies); many lack a sense of meaning in their philosophies, and the concept of happiness as an obligation is missing. Their emphasis is on hedonism, while the Torah emphasis is on *simchah shel mitzvah* (the joy of good deeds) and the development of gratitude for all that we have."

Rabbi Zelig Pliskin

How to Love Each Other as Ourselves

"The command to love your neighbor as yourself (Leviticus 19:18) has tiers of meaning. First, love is a biblical obligation. If it were not, then we'd be told 'to try to love your neighbor.' The G-d of the Bible claims we can actually learn to love. Too often we equate love with infatuation. We can't force ourselves to become infatuated with another person. But love can be learned, and not surprisingly, since G-d wants to engender this love among us, the Bible hints at how to succeed in this quest.

Biblical Jacob wanted to marry his first true love, Rachel. But his wily father-in-law tricked Jacob, and he married Rachel's sister, Leah, instead. After the traditional week-long celebration of the marriage, Jacob was finally permitted to marry Rachel. And with that, we are informed, 'and he (Jacob) also went into Rachel and also loved Rachel' (Genesis 29:30). Why 'also loved'? Jacob always loved Rachel, so why is the Bible telling us that he 'also loved Rachel'? The 'also loved' comes to teach us that in the week Jacob had spent with Leah, he had realized Leah's virtues and in doing so learned to love her as well, even though Jacob was well aware that Leah, like most of us, was not perfect: 'Leah's eyes were weak' (29:17).

'Hear, Israel, the Eternal our G-d, the Eternal is One. And you shall love the Eternal your G-d with all your heart, with all your soul and with all your might' (Deuteronomy 6:4-5). That love should be the central point of all biblical goals, second only to the understanding of the Unity of existence, is quite simply extraordinary. These two primary verses of the Bible tell us what the G-d of the Bible wants from and for Its creations. Love implies society, not isolation on a mountaintop abstractly contemplating the meaning of life. The biblical statement, 'And G-d said: It is not good for man to be alone' (Genesis 2:18), speaks of the centrality that human relationships occupy in G-d's plan of the world. Similarly, 'Behold how good and pleasant it is when brethren dwell also together' (Psalms 133:1). Together. We fulfil one of G-d's basic designs through our relations with others.

'You shall love your neighbor as yourself: *I am the Eternal G-d'* (Leviticus 19:18). Through the Bible, G-d has informed us that when you can truly love another, not for what you can get but rather for what you can give, then a third partner joins with you in that friendship, the King of kings. According to the Bible, G-d tells us that if you want to build a loving relationship with G-d, start by loving other members of humanity, all of whom are made in G-d's image.

Friendship, how we relate to others, is the biblical measure of how we relate to G-d and how G-d relates to us. As bizarre as it seems, G-d wants our love and friendship. And that love and friendship can only be expressed through our relations with others. We are the spiritual image of G-d on earth."

GERALD SCHROEDER

"The potency of the language of Torah is a vast subject. Hebrew is called the 'holy language' because it underlies all of manifest reality.

The root concept is that *the world was created by means of the language*; the world was 'spoken' into existence. When the Torah states 'And G-d said...' in creating, it does not mean He gave instruction; it means He spoke a word and that word condensed, crystallized, concretized into the object it denotes. In reality, Hebrew words do not describe things, they *are* the things themselves.

In Hebrew, unlike other languages, the word for a 'word' and the word for a 'thing' are the same – the word *davar* means both 'word' and 'thing' because in essence any thing is none other than the word the Torah uses to create the thing. (Of course, this principle has a corollary – all things in the world are speaking their words, the world is created to be a dialog; we should be listening.)

The Torah is a film through which an ineffable light is shone; the light shines through the Torah and projects onto a screen which is the world we experience. The Torah is the film, the fabric of our reality is the image on the screen. Each detail on the film is projected onto the screen; each word in the Torah is a thing in the world. (Each is enough to fathom the other – one who knows the Torah will know the world; one who knows the world will know the Torah.) No other language has a hint of this; in the languages of the world, words connote things by convention, that is all.

There is another dimension to the Hebrew language too, that of *gematria*. This is the numerical correlate of the verbal element; the letters have a system of numerical equivalents that parallel their literate function. This means that a Hebrew word speaks its meaning both explicitly and mathematically; in a sense like the two functions of human expression and scientific (or mathematical) notation of other cultures. The wonder here is that the two systems overlay each other: in English, you might express an idea verbally in characters of the English alphabet or choose to express the same idea in mathematical notation using Arabic numerals: in Hebrew however, the letters and the numerals are co-extensive. The *same letters* do both; a Hebrew word expresses the verbal aspect of an idea and the *same word* read as a numeric expression gives the mathematical or quantitative aspect of the idea.

The Hebrew word for 'one,' *echad* is comprised of letters whose numerical total is thirteen. The Hebrew word for 'love,' *ahavah* has a numerical value of thirteen – love means the coming together of parts to form one.

Since Judaism defines the quality of relationships in terms of giving and primarily the giving of self, it follows that the intensity and meaning of my relationship with you exist only to the extent that there is a value of self that I have to give. If I am empty I have nothing to give, and if I have nothing to give, no real relationship can exist between us.

So the development of self is primary, both intrinsically and in forming the root of relationships with others.

In the idea of love this comes into sharp focus. In Jewish spiritual thinking love is defined, perhaps paradoxically at first sight, in terms of self. Love of self is the primary mode of being in the healthy psyche, the drive for self-preservation relates to this, and it is the entirely natural state. This is deeply related to the only direct and immediate knowledge, the knowledge of self. There is a deep connection between love and inner knowledge (remember that the Torah's term for marital love is 'knowledge').

The key is this: real love is not love that I have for you as *distinct* from me, but rather, my love for you is an *expansion or extension of myself to include you*. (This is the depth in 'Love your neighbor as yourself.')

Genuine love of another exists when that other is included in the ambit of one's own being. When I have maturity and depth to expand my grasp of myself to include you, when you become integral to my definition of myself, when you are as close to me as I am to myself, then my love for you follows automatically. I love you because at a deep level we have become indiscernible as two; we are one.

Love is not simply where two meet and share; that is mere partnership. Love is generated in the process of two becoming one. Expanding the sense of self to include another is the ultimate act of love; nothing beyond that step is needed."

RABBI AKIVA TATZ

What can be more beautiful than hearing how Rabbi Shlomo Carlebach describes the true sublime nature of love?

"Listen to me, sweetest friends. Just to talk about loving people, loving G-d, about healing people, you touch the center of the world, the center of life. Because, what is the most G-dlike thing you can do to another human being?

How does G-d give us life? Rav Nachman calls it 'noam elyon' - high sweetness. There is nothing sweeter in the world than loving somebody. Even in this world, it's sweet. Rav Nachman says that heavenly sweetness is coming down into this world every second, every billionth of a second. It's flowing down. The only thing is, you must have the sense to pick it up.

There are two kinds of love in the world. can you imagine, I am walking down the street, don't feel any love in my heart, not hatred, not love - nothing. Suddenly, I meet a very beautiful girl and I fall in love with her. That means, I needed something to touch me, to bring about that I suddenly have felt love. This is the love after Creation.

The Torah says, in Psalms, 'olam chesed yebaneh' - G-d created the world with love. That does not mean that there is a world, and G-d loves that world. That is already the love after Creation. It means, G-d had so much love in His heart that He had to create the world.

Let's talk about children. There are two kinds of love you have for children. There is a love of after they are born; they're born, they are your children, and you love them. But, you only created them because you have so much love in your heart. This is like the love of before Creation.

Imagine, some people just get together without loving each other, and children are born. They are so angry, because they are missing the most important part - you only create with love, because G-d created the world with love.

Now, I want you to know the deepest depths. Remember, when G-d made a covenant with our father Abraham, Abraham circumcised himself, and on the third day, he was really in pain. The Talmud says that the third day is somewhat dangerous. So, the sun came out very strong, and there were no guests. Abraham sent his servants to find him a guest. How can one live without guests in his house? But, there were no guests. So, three angels came.

Abraham was welcoming guests all his life, the kind of guests who really needed to eat and to sleep. The Torah, however, does not record that. The Torah records that he took in three angels, who really didn't need to eat. The Talmud says that they just pretended they were eating.

Abraham, after he entered the Covenant with G-d, didn't need a poor man to bring out the love in him, which is the love after Creation. After he entered the Covenant with G-d, he was so G-dlike, he just had to do good, like G-d. He was not in a state where, if you see a person you love them, you see a poor man and want to give him food. He was looking for a poor man. He was looking to love somebody.

The Talmud says that G-d came to heal Avraham; that means that G-d came to give him the secret of healing. Because, if you remember, the Covenant with Noah was only that the world will always exist. Noah was not concerned with how many people will live and how many will die - as long as there will always be a world, there will be survivors. The Covenant with Abraham was that someday the world will be fixed, some day the world will be healed, the world will be cured. So, after G-d made the Covenant with Abraham, G-d came to give him the secret of healing. The secret of healing is like creating the world

There has to be not the kind of love there is after Creation. There has to be the kind of love before Creation.

G-d has many names. G-d has the name **HaShem**, and the name **Elokim**. 'In the beginning, Elokim created...' This is basically the name of justice, of sternness. There has to be **Elokim**, there has to be order - day is day, night is night, winter is winter; there must be order in the universe. When candle-lighting is 4:20, there is nothing you can do about it that's when it is. You cannot say, listen, I will be able to feel Shabbos better if I rest now and kindle the lights later. You cannot change when Shabbos is. You cannot say, 'I am living by the name of **HaShem**, I am infinite.' You are not infinite. Don't kid yourself. G-d is infinite. The world is not infinite. You are not infinite.

But again, the other side. The finite people are so disgusting, Gevalt, are they disgusting. They are murderers. You can kill somebody. You can say, 'This person is a thief - put him in prison. He did this - shoot him.' No mercy. The deepest secret of life is that you have to keep both together. There has to be Absolute order, and also the infinite. Both together. When it comes to educating children, you have to be **HaShem Elokim**. You teach them Day is Day, Night is Night. But, on the other hand, if that is all you teach them, you cripple them. You kill G-d's name, **HaShem**, inside of them, that infinite name of G-d. You have to teach them both.

G-d forbid, if somebody is sick, he is sick. Have you ever heard people whisper that if somebody is sick, he probably deserves it?

People have excuses, people give lectures on why the six million had to be killed. Who are these people? They are murderers! They may not kill people, but they have murder in their hearts.

What is their problem?
They are not connected to G-d's infinite name.

Sometimes, we love somebody in a measured love. We want to know how much money her family has, how many degrees she has. This is not love in an infinite way. This is not the love before Creation. Before Creation there was nothing, except for G-d's infinite love. There was nothing else. Only the infinite.

When you want to cure somebody who is sick, you cannot cure a person with the love of after Creation. When somebody is in pain, somebody is crying, and you tell them they are wrong, you think now is the time to educate them? Especially little children. The adults say: 'Why are you crying? Your father hit you? He was probably right.' Sure, he was right. But, if I talk this way to a child, I can't cure her. I make her sicker. You have to connect them with

G-d's name that existed before there was anything in the world. When I want to cure somebody, it has to be on the level of before Creation. There is nothing there - and there is everything.

I want to talk about healing with hands. Basically, our hands are finite. How much can you do with your hands? Everything you can do with them is finite. True? No, it isn't true. Words are finite. Imagine, I tell a girl I love her very much. So, I told her, with finite words. But, imagine, if, while I tell her, I hold her hand. The hands have the power of giving over something infinite.

The Talmud says that G-d created the world with His hands. There are the hands of before Creation. The hands of before Creation don't know of any limits, don't know of anything finite. The hands of before Creation don't do anything wrong, It's impossible. On such a high level, evil doesn't exist.

If I love a girl very much, and I find out she is not so good, and I decide I won't see her anymore, the problem is not that she is bad, but that I don't really love her so much. If whatever she did wrong can destroy my love, then my love wasn't so strong! But, if I really love her, and someone says; 'Listen, she is a terrible girl', I would say: 'I don't care.' It doesn't mean that I don't care for her being wrong, but that her doing wrong doesn't reach the place where I love her. My love is so high, that the wrong she did remains lower, and doesn't reach the love.

So, there are the hands of before Creation, and there are the hands of after Creation, and there are the hands of Mashiach. 'Mikdash HaShem Konenu Yadecha' – 'The Temple of G-d, Your hands will fashion.' The first two temples were built by us, by human beings. The third temple, for which we are waiting, will be rebuilt just by G-d's hands. Suddenly, it will appear.

There is a kind of healing and there is a kind of love, which takes time. G-d created the world in six days. In six days! But then, sometimes G-d's hands heal in one second. So, there are two kinds of healing. There is the healing of the six days of Creation. With all the being infinite, it still took six days. When the Messiah comes, the hands that will rebuild the holy temple will do so in a second. When you love somebody very much, you can hold their hand and they will sense if it is the hands of before Creation, or the hands after Creation, or, are they the hands of Mashiach? Or the third temple? Children are carried in one's hands; they are so connected to hands. Some children grow up with the hands of after Creation, and some grow up with the hand of when Mashiach is coming.

Have you ever seen sometimes when a child is crying, and you pat her head and try to soothe her, and she still cries? Sometimes, you put your hands on her head, and she stops crying. It doesn't take any time - she is suddenly smiling. It is Mashiach's hands. It doesn't take any time.

Some people do not have even a taste of the Infinite. Do you know who are the lonely, broken people? They don't have a taste of the All.

Some people don't have the All, but, for once in their lives, they had a taste of the All.

Imagine, I love my wife very much, and I buy her an apartment in New York one in Paris, one in Israel. I give her a lot of things. One day, I was praying at the Holy Wall, and, while I was praying, a little stone fell down from one of the Holy stones. I picked it up, and I brought my wife that stone. This is All. So much deeper.

Sometimes, I give my child many things. But, where is the All?

The Talmud says that G-d's presence, the Shechinah, is above the head of a sick person. This has millions of meanings. When a person is sick, what do they need? They don't need little things. They need the All.

When it comes to words, you can only utter one word after another. When it comes to hearing, you can only hear one thing at a time. The Gemara says, 'Trei Kolei Lo Nishma'in' – two voices cannot be heard clearly at the same time. You can hear only one word after another, one voice after another. But, when it comes to seeing, you can see many things at once. Seeing is connected to the All.

When do people cry? When I miss particulars, I don't cry. When it touches my All, my eyes, then I cry. When you love somebody very much, you look in their eyes. You don't look at their ears, only their eyes. Eyes are so deep. With some people, when you look at their eyes, you see only dollar bills. With others, when you look in their eyes, you see G-d's presence.

This is an Ishbitzer Torah. Animals eat exactly what they need - they don't overeat. Why is it that we human beings don't know limits, not only in food, but in everything? Why is that? Because spiritually, I can reach beyond myself. What is so special about this world? In this world, everything is open. So much so that yesterday, although I was the lowest person in the world, today I can reach the highest level. Although yesterday I had a fight with someone. Today we can be great friends. This world has something that is not finite. If you ever thought that heaven is infinite, you are mistaken. Heaven has the finiteness of heaven. Heaven is also finite. You know what really is infinite? This world! Right here, in the chair we are sitting on - this world is infinite.

There's another Torah from the Ishbitzer. The Ishbitzer says, the soul in heaven, before I was, when I was dwelling in heaven, was beautiful, but - who needed me? Nobody needed me, and I didn't need anybody else. In heaven, who needs friends? Friends can't do anything for you. But, only in this world can you be a friend to somebody, and somebody can be a friend to you. Some days, I can walk on the street and hear somebody cry, and you know where I can reach in one second? Beyond myself. Let's assume if I work hard, I can reach a certain spiritual height. Let's say I'll be a million miles high. But then, there can be one moment when I am eternally high – beyond everything. So, the Ishbitzer says, every person has an absolute drive to reach beyond, to be infinite. The only thing is - if I don't know how to handle it, I want more food, more money, more clothes. You have this drive. The question is, there is 'le-eiteh' - stuffing. What are you stuffing yourself with - to be a better friend, to love people more, or are you stuffing yourself with yet another good time? So, he says, what HaShem did was to take a Tzaddik, a holy man, and put him in charge of 'le-eiteh.' What are holy people doing in the world? To let the world know, don't put your drive for the infinite in stupid things. You should be searching for that absolute stuffing yourself, reaching beyond yourself, every second.

When somebody is sick, they get in touch with the deepest depths of their life. What are they missing? If you ask a sick person if he wants to live, he'll say yes. Why does he want to live? He is crying, why didn't I reach beyond myself? I had such an opportunity, why didn't I do that? Why wasn't I infinite?

What are friends for? What does it mean to love somebody? It means that that person puts me in touch with the Infinite, to reach beyond myself.

A wedding begins when the groom covers the face of the bride. That means he is telling the bride that, because of her, he is becoming infinite. The eyes are infinite. I can reach even beyond the All; what I thought was All, is not.

When somebody is sick, the Torah says, our holy fathers had 'bakol mikol kol' - they had the All. You know what Avraham taught the world? Before Avraham, there were a lot of holy people, but they taught the world that you can reach beyond yourself. Avraham is 'bakol mikol kol', deeper. If you have the All, you are so full. If you have everything in the world, but the All is missing, gevalt are you empty. You are aching.

I have seen people who have everything - family, money. But, they are broken. I have seen people who have nothing, no money, but they have the All, they can reach beyond themselves.

When Jacob had a dream, he dreamt that there is a ladder going up to heaven. A ladder is finite - it has a beginning and an end. Even heaven is finite. But, then he saw 'Vehinei HaShem Nitzav Alav' - G-d was standing above him. Do you know what he saw? That you can reach beyond yourself. You can do one thing, and suddenly, you are something else.

When we see people crying, at that moment they are open for the All. At that moment, they are ready to reach beyond themselves. When the Holy Temple was destroyed, it says 'Aynai, Aynai, yorda mayim' - my eyes can't stop crying. What is the Temple all about? How can G-d be limited to one place?

There are many people who say, 'I am infinite I cannot limit myself to one religion.' What's their problem? Between Infinite nothing and Infinite something, there is such a thin line. Gevalt, is it thin.

You know, when you love somebody very much, you sit under a tree for an hour, and you know what you experience? Not the infiniteness of heaven, but G-d's infiniteness, which is only in this world. You can do a favor to one person, just be close to one person, and see what you experience; G-d's infiniteness, which is only in this world. Esau comes to us and says, let's face it, you know what G-d is all about? Do this, do that. He is holding a stick over us. I can't stand G-d's stick. G-d makes me so finite. In order to get out of it, I stuff myself. You know what to answer him back? You want to be infinite? When you pass by a street, and see one poor man dying from hunger, give him all the money you have. Be Infinite - just one person. When you pray to G-d, don't look at the clock. Be Infinite.

When you have a chance to heal one person, you are not healing just one person. It's not finite. At that moment you can reach beyond yourself, reaching that love of G-d which was before Creation. Infinite. When you walk up to a person and give them a good word, when someone is heartbroken and you give them a good word, when you utter some words - sometimes they are your words, sometimes they are Mashiach's words. In one second, you can cure that person, you can give him back his self-confidence.

The world understands today that you cannot cure the body without the soul. What does that mean? You cannot cure their finite parts if you also cannot cure their infiniteness.

What is my soul? My soul has this deep longing, because my soul knows that I am here in this world to reach beyond myself. I want something so deep, so glorious.

You know friends, sometimes children are so angry at their parents, because all their parents talk to them about is the finite part of them - be a doctor, make money, have two cars. Children feel, how come you never talk to me about something deep, something holy? Where is the Infinite?

Sometimes, parents and children have those moments that are just Infinite.

You know, it is possible that somebody gives me a million dollars. I like them. But, one person gave me one handshake, and I love him forever, because, the million dollars was finite - the handshake was infinite.

You know, sweetest friends, the closer we get to Mashiach's coming, the stronger the desire gets to reach beyond ourselves.

Basically, medicine is the most finite science in the world. Somebody's body is sick you cure the body. If the feet are sick, you cure the feet. Now, something is happening to the world. They feel that if the feet are sick, the pain is felt not just in the feet, but all over. The whole person must be cured, not just the feet. I can walk with my feet two blocks, and I was finite. I can walk with my feet to do somebody a favor and I was Infinite.

You know, friends, sometimes a person needs just a finite friendship. Sometimes a person absolutely needs an infinite friendship. Sometimes children come home from school and they need just a peanut butter sandwich. Sometimes, they need an infinite peanut butter sandwich.

The deepest secret of life is, if you are connected to a person only on the level of after Creation - you don't get it. If you are connected to them on the level of before Creation, you have a Covenant with G-d, you are like Avraham Avinu.

Before Abraham entered the Covenant with G-d, Covenant meaning I am completely given over to G-d in an infinite way, to serve G-d every second - before Avraham entered the Covenant he knew that if he saw a poor person he had to give them food, and a place to stay.

After the Covenant, he had a different kind of welcoming guests. He knew that if a person has no home, he needs more than a place to stay. He knew that a person who has nothing needs everything. Suddenly, Avraham Avinu realized that a person who has no home, nothing, has vessels to receive everything. And, when the angels who were greeted by Avraham told him that he will have children, suddenly Avraham realized that a child needs everything, everything.

I want to bless you and I want to bless all the people who heal people. We are all sick. When a person is, G-d forbid, a little bit sick, when things go wrong in our lives - at that moment, we have a vessel for everything. It says of the Holy Land: 'Eretz kol bo' - a land that has everything. We were 2,000 years in exile, and G-d didn't give the Holy Land back to us. You know when we suddenly had vessels for the Holy Land? When we walked through gas chambers. We had nothing any more. There was nothing left. Nothing. We have to see the Holy Land - G-d should give it to us completely. We still think we have something, we think we have Western civilization, we have the U.S.A., - we really have nothing. We have only G-d. The moment we have nothing, we become a vessel for everything.

When I have Shabbos, I don't want a little Shabbos, I want the All of Shabbos – 'Yom Shekulo Shabbos' - a day that is All of Shabbos.

We don't need friends just to say hi to. We need friends who are infinite friends. Today we have a chance. G-d opens gates to us. We can reach beyond ourselves.

Remember, Rav Kook says, the sign that Mashiach is coming is that our children are so beautiful. The children coming down from heaven now are so beautiful, so special. We have to give them All. I want to bless you and me. There are so many children running around in the world, whose parents don't have the faintest idea what All is. You and I have to be G-d's messengers. We say, 'Refaeinu HaShem Venerafeh' – 'G-d, heal me.' I want to be healed on a G-d level. When something hurts me, I don't want just to cure my body. I want to cure my life.

A lot of times, we have these infinite moments. But, we are still living in a finite world. There is day, there is night, I have to make a living. I have to go to work. The saddest thing is, we don't incorporate these infinite moments into our finite lives.

Many people stand by the Holy Wall and cry their eyes out. At that moment, they are infinitely Jewish. But, when they come back, they go back to the way they were. Their *Elokim* and their *HaShem* don't work together. Because we are finite, G-d created a finite world. G-d wants something more from us, even deeper. Mashiach is coming. G-d's name that will be in the world will be *Ekeyeh asher Ekeyeh* – 'I will be what I will be.' This means, not finite and not infinite. It's deeper than that.

I want to bless you and me and all of us, when we are learning, we learn one page, but let that page be infinite. But, I want to hold the page in my hands, it's finite, it's one page, but it's infinite. A love letter is just a page but, it's really infinite. It's everything.

The world is so broken. The world has vessels for the unbelievable things that are happening. If only all the doctors, all the psychiatrists, would have enough sense, and maybe someday they will, to fix the All, really to fix, to give people the strength to reach beyond themselves ... Children want to reach beyond themselves. If you don't tell your children that they are the most beautiful in the world - don't talk to them. Then you'll tell me, but, what about my neighbor's child? She is also beautiful. Ah, on a finite level, it's a contradiction, but on an infinite level, my child is the most beautiful in the world, your child is the most beautiful in the world, for G-d, every human being is the most beautiful in the world. Maybe one day we shall know that all of us, every single one of us, is the best in the whole world.

***

You meet sometimes people who love each other, and you watch them. Do they make each other whole? Do they break each other's heart? Ah, then it's for real. And if they don't break each other's heart anymore, if their heart doesn't stop beating in each other's presence, then it's meaningless.

Once a year there was a collection for the sacrifice of the Holy Temple. And everybody was giving half a shekel, a broken shekel, and this is what kept the Temple going. You know what we're telling each other. It breaks my heart to know that I can bring something to the Holy Temple.

***

Love cannot be taught. All we can hope for is that we should unlearn all the hatred. Because hatred is taught. Love is from heaven.

***

In Psalms it says, 'G-d created the world with love.' That doesn't mean that there is a world, and G-d loves the world. It means that G-d has so much love, that G-d had to create the world. Imagine some people just get together without loving each other, and then a baby is born. Why are they all so angry? Because they are missing the most important part—you only create with love because G-d created the world with love."

MEDITATION and PRAYER

Rabbi Aryeh Kaplan writes: "The Hebrew word for meditation is *hitbodedut* (התבודדות). The word occurs in this context in Judaic writings spanning over a thousand years, and is used for all the various forms of Jewish meditation. Yet, in most people's minds, it is primarily with Rabbi Nachman of Breslov (1772-1810) that this word is associated.

Many types of meditation were used by Jewish saints and mystics. A vast wealth of ancient literature describes how the prophets of Israel used meditation to reach their high spiritual states.

In an important teaching, the Talmud states, 'One who prays must direct his eyes downward and his heart on high.' One of the important commentators, Rabbi Yonah Gerondi (1196-1263) explains, 'This means that in one's heart, he should imagine that he is standing in heaven. He must banish all worldly delight and bodily enjoyment from his heart. The early sages taught that if one wishes to have true concentration (*kavanah*), he must divest his body from his soul.'

A few decades later, this was expressed even more explicitly by the great codifier Rabbi Yaakov ben Asher (1270-1343) in his *Tur*. Speaking of "saints and men of deeds", he writes 'they would meditate (*hitboded)* and concentrate on their prayers until they reached a level where they would be divested of the physical. The transcendental spirit would be strengthened in them until they would reach a level close to prophecy.' This passage is quoted verbatim by Yosef Karo (1488-1575) in his *Shulchan Aruch,* the standard code of Jewish law.

Although hitbodedut denotes meditation, as Rabbi Nachman saw it, it was also a form of personal prayer. Indeed, that is how most contemporary Breslover Chasidim see it. It is seen not so much as a means to attain higher states of consciousness, but as a means to self-perfection. If a person is constantly conversing with G-d, he is certain to become more G-dly, he is sure to have a greater desire to do G-d's will.

Beyond that, constant personal prayer is seen as a means to a good life, even here on earth. When a person discusses his problems with a friend, they no longer seem so formidable. If one can learn to discuss them with G-d, they virtually shrink to insignificance. As one Breslover Chasid put it, 'When you bring your problems to G-d, they cease to exist. There is nothing in the world to worry about.' Or as King David expressed it almost three millennia ago, 'Place your burden on G-d, and He will carry (it for) you.' (Psalms 55:23)."

For those wishing to practice hitbodedut, the meditation and personal prayer best described by Rebbe Nachman, a fine comprehensive guide is given by Rabbi Avraham Greenbaum:

Hitbodedut: Time for Yourself

"The literal meaning of the Hebrew word *hitbodedut* is "making oneself alone". The aim is not to become a hermit. In essence, hitbodedut is private time that you put aside for yourself on a regular basis. You detach yourself from your normal routine for a while in order to explore and develop yourself through meditation, introspection, self-expression, talking, praying, singing and any other method that helps you.

Hitbodedut is alluded to in various places in the Bible. In different forms it was taught by many spiritual teachers throughout the ages. It was given special emphasis by Rebbe Nachman of Breslov. Some of the main techniques that may be used in hitbodedut are discussed in more detail below.

The mark of a successful hitbodedut session is that you should feel better than before! Sometimes this is achieved through relaxation, breathing, settling the mind, etc. At other times more active methods may be employed, as described later.

The hitbodedut session itself may not necessarily be calm throughout. In one and the same session you may go through a whole gamut of different experiences, from heightened consciousness, insight, joy, gratitude, peace of mind and divine connection to frustration, inner pain, grief, tears and many more. Be willing to face negative aspects of yourself and your life honestly and with the confidence that G-d can help you discover the good concealed within negativity and darkness. Searching for this goodness will bring you to greater harmony and joy.

Aim to set aside time for yourself every day. This could be anywhere from about ten minutes to as much as an hour, according to your needs.

When and where

Choose a time when you are not likely to be disturbed. Many people prefer to practice hitbodedut early in the morning before all the pressures of the day build up. Some take a break for hitbodedut between activities. Others practice hitbodedut at the end of the day, finding that it helps them unwind. For best results, choose a time when have not just eaten a large meal as this may interfere with your mental clarity. If you are unable to sleep at night, you may try hitbodedut then.

If possible, find a place where you can have some privacy. If you are confined to bed, you can practice hitbodedut right there. If you are up and about choose a quiet corner whether at home or elsewhere. Natural surroundings can be especially conducive to calm and spirituality. If you have full access to a suitable natural spot, or even your own back yard, take full advantage of it!

Before you begin a session of hitbodedut, it is a good idea to decide in advance how long you want the session to last, e.g. fifteen minutes, half an hour, etc. Have a clock or timer handy.

Make yourself as comfortable as possible. There is no required posture for hitbodedut. Choose a posture that you find conducive to relaxation and clarity. Many people find it best to practice hitbodedut sitting in a comfortable chair with the back well supported. If you wish, you may stand or walk about. Lying down is acceptable, especially if you are tired or not feeling well. However at other times lying down is not recommended as it may make you drowsy.

Now you are ready to begin.

Settling the mind

Simply sitting quietly in a relaxed state can free your mind and help you get in touch with your thoughts, feelings and creative powers. One by one you let go of your tensions and they drop away, leaving you with a blessed feeling of profound calm, liberation, clarity, enhanced sensitivity and alertness. It becomes easier to think, understand, remember things and work out problems. New insights may result, together with a growing awareness of the spiritual dimension of life.

The benefits of deep relaxation are so great that it is well worth spending a little time learning the technique. Initially, you may have to concentrate more on bodily relaxation. Once you have mastered this, you will be able to enter a relaxed state virtually at will and have full enjoyment of the mental, emotional and spiritual benefits it can bring.

If you wish, start with a few stretches. If you are confined to bed, you can practice lying down. Otherwise sit erect with your head comfortably balanced and your eyes closed. Focus your attention on the different parts of your body in order, one by one, from the feet upwards. Which muscles are tense? The key to relaxing is to understand that no effort is called for. Simply let go of tension. If you become restless, stretch and move around a bit, or take a few deep breaths, and then go back to quietly sitting.

To relax deeply, you must also let go of the inner fear, anxiety, anger and resentment and other factors that so often cause people to tense various parts of their bodies. The way to overcome fear is by having faith that everything in your life is in G-d's hands, and G-d is good and wants your good.

The active phase of hitbodedut

Some people hold that within each individual there are natural wellsprings of vitality and joy ready and waiting to flow forth, and if you can only relax and settle your mind sufficiently, the happiness will naturally bubble up within you.

However, this fails to take account how hurt, wounded, thwarted and stunted many people are inside as a result of what they have been through in their lives. This is why some people find that when they start meditating, disturbing thoughts and feelings begin to surface, or they feel gray and cloudy and want to go to sleep.

In order to draw out, nurture and actualize the true power of your inner "point", it is not sufficient merely to relax and try to settle the mind. It is also necessary to work on yourself actively in order to overcome inner forces that may be inhibiting this latent power.

After an initial period of quiet sitting, a typical hitbodedut session turns into a workshop in which you contemplate what is happening in your life as a whole. Then you actively start working on yourself in order to change and grow.

The power of words

Your most powerful tool for change, growth and spiritual connection is right under your nose. It is your mouth. Just as you can influence others by the way you speak to them, so you can affect your own self. With the right words, songs, cries and other means of expression, you can influence your own states of mind and direct yourself to where you want to go.

Small children quite innocently express themselves out loud – to G-d, to themselves, to invented characters, or to no-one in particular. But as we grow older this easy self-expression tends to become muted, turning into the continual, and often negative, internal dialogs within our minds. Sometimes our innermost thoughts and feelings go underground and may be hidden from our very selves.

Talking to yourself is popularly considered a sign of madness. Perhaps it is when the person is not in control of it. But one of the sanest things you can do to enhance your life is to relearn the art of self-expression and consciously use words to focus your mind, to make contact with the different sides of yourself, to direct yourself and to talk deep into your soul and right out to G-d.

To whom are you really talking in hitbodedut – to yourself or to G-d? The truth is that even when you talk "to yourself," you are really talking to G-d. Although you experience yourself as an independent entity, at root your vitality as a living being derives from G-d, as does everything else in the world. All your thoughts and feelings ultimately come from G-d, even though they are channelled to you via the mysterious entity we call the "self" or "soul," which makes them seem to originate "inside" you.

In order to make fresh changes in your life and grow, you must find new inner power. Fresh energy, positive mental states, insights and original ideas are all new creations that ultimately come from G-d, the Supreme Source of all creation. In hitbodedut you consciously reach out to G-d with words, songs, cries and the like in order to channel new life into yourself. When you "talk to yourself" in hitbodedut, you are at the point of encounter between your everyday self and the Supreme Power from which you your very life derives.

Don't be embarrassed. You are alone and no-one can hear you. Find your own voice! Don't worry if you feel you don't know what to say. Everybody has this experience at first. Experiment with different kinds of self-expression until you discover those that have meaning for you.

By definition hitbodedut is a highly individual practice. You are completely unique. You must find your own way to connect to your inner "point" and with G-d. Tailor your hitbodedut to your own personal needs. You may use different techniques at different times depending on your mood and your needs at the moment.

Hitbodedut Techniques

Guide Words

These are words or phrases of your choice that you repeat aloud and over and over in hitbodedut in order to evoke a desired state of mind, focus your thoughts, etc. Saying words aloud or in a whisper is much more powerful than merely thinking them in your mind. Repeating the word Shalom, "Peace," can help calm you if you are tense. When you want to make changes in your life or achieve important goals, keep yourself on track with guide words that express exactly what you want, (e.g. "Relax!" "Patience!" "Kindness!" "Moderation!") To develop a deeper spiritual connection, try simply repeating "G-d" or some other name for the Higher Power that has special meaning for you.

Melody

Singing or humming the right song is a powerful way to guide yourself and influence your moods and states of mind. If you are feeling uninspired, negative or depressed, choose a melody with a positive energy. When you first begin humming even a favourite song, it may take some effort to get into the right spirit. But if you persist and sing it over and over again, you will find that the melody will begin to lift you. It will bring healing rhythms into your soul, your mind and your very body. The melodies taught by outstanding spiritual teachers have the power to lift people to exalted states of consciousness and to inculcate deeper faith and trust.

Affirmations

Events, circumstances, other people and certain forces within ourselves often conspire to make us lose sight of essential truths. An affirmation is a statement of some important truth or belief about yourself, your goals and values, or about life in general. For example, "My goal is to heal and to live life to the full every day, every moment," or "I believe in G-d, and G-d is good," etc. Regularly making such affirmations out loud keeps these truths at the forefront of your mind. Develop your own set of affirmations about your beliefs, goals and ideals, or choose some inspiring quotations. Say them out loud regularly in your hitbodedut sessions.

Guiding Questions

If you want to use hitbodedut to explore yourself and resolve certain issues in your life, give focus to your quest by asking yourself guiding questions, such as "What is on my mind?" "What am I really feeling? "Where in the world am I?" "What is my purpose in life?" "What do I really want?" "How can I attain it?" "What keeps me locked into destructive patterns?" "What are my positive points?" etc. Asking such questions out loud can aid your concentration when exploring various issues and can help you develop new answers.

Self-Expression

As you ask yourself guiding questions, many different thoughts and feelings are likely to pass through your mind. In order to understand yourself better, express what you are thinking and feeling out loud. Try to articulate your thoughts and feelings as clearly as you can. Listen carefully to what you are saying. Often we are in conflict within ourselves. Articulating the different sides of our personalities can help us explore and resolve inner conflicts. Give honest expression to all aspects of yourself, and especially to your highest ideals and aspirations. To give continuity to your mental and spiritual growth, it can be useful to jot down the ideas and insights that come to you in hitbodedut and keep them in a special file.

Cries and Tears

Little children naturally cry out in pain and hurt. You too are allowed to cry out because of your pain and to complain about the things that are troubling you. Cry to G-d about the pain in your body and soul. Cry out about your fears. Weep over your deepest hurt and sorrow. Weep for yourself. Weep for your dear ones. Weep for the world. For many people a cry of pain or an unarticulated sob rising from the depths of the heart can be their first act of outreach to G-d. "Where are You? G-d please help me! Please help!!!"

Thanks

Don't dwell only on the negative. Think about all the good things too! If you can see, hear, taste, feel… thank G-d for it. Express your thanks out loud. "Thank you, G-d, that I am breathing, thinking… I may not be well, but I am alive! I've had good times, I've done good things…" List the good things in your life. Count your blessings and thank G-d for them. People often associate prayer with making requests to G-d. But before you start asking G-d for what you need, first give thanks for all the gifts and blessings you already enjoy in your life. Make a habit to speak to G-d about all the different aspects of your life.

Requests

List your prayers and requests. Even if some of them seem unrealistic, for G-d anything is possible. Make detailed requests: e.g. "Please send healing to my arm, my leg, my heart, my lungs, my kidneys, etc. Help me work on my lack of self-confidence, low self-esteem, anger, pessimism, etc. Help me in my relationship with so and so. Help me in that situation at home or at work, etc." Pray for the joy and the will to live. Ask for insight and enlightenment. Put your dreams and your deepest yearnings into words, and ask G-d to help you attain what you want.

Psalms and Prayers

If you find yourself unable to express yourself to G-d or you feel that your own words are inadequate, open the Siddur (Jewish Prayer Book) or the Psalms. These are rich spiritual treasures containing prayers of many different kinds, expressing every mood and need in life. If you wish, open them at random and read until you find a passage that has a special meaning for you. When you find such a passage, say it out loud, even several times. Leave marks in the book so that you can easily find your favourite passage again.

Hitbodedut and Growth

Make use of the different techniques of hitbodedut according to your own personal needs each day. Life is constantly changing. New things are always happening. Our bodily states fluctuate from day to day. Our moods and our thoughts shift from minute to minute. For this reason, hitbodedut is different each time you do it.

Some people may want to launch immediately into the more active forms of self-expression such as talking directly to G-d. For others, quiet sitting and contemplation may often be the prime element in their hitbodedut.

No matter where you choose to put your focus, the most important thing is to practice hitbodedut regularly. The effects are cumulative. As you practice, you'll gain experience and learn how to make use of different techniques as appropriate in order to grow and accomplish what you want.

Use hitbodedut as part of your self-healing, or to work on specific problem areas in your life, whether within yourself, in your relationships, at home, in your work, in the wider community, etc. Use guiding questions and self-expression to define and understand your problems and obstacles.

Whether you want to heal yourself, make a change of lifestyle, attitudes, outlook, etc., or accomplish any other goal starts off as an idea in your mind. In order to turn the potential idea into an actual accomplishment, you must first develop a clear understanding of what you will have to do, step by step, in order to attain it. Then you must actually take the next step.

Hitbodedut is the time to do this work of clarifying your ideas and working out strategies for attaining your goals. The way to do it is with words. Articulate what it is you really want. Try to define the obstacles and difficulties you face. Express out loud your various ideas as to how you can overcome your problems. When you express your thoughts as clearly as possible, you can begin to see where your ideas may need further clarification.

What is up to you to do and what is up to G-d? Many things are in G-d's hands alone. All you can do is pray about them – again and again. Even when it comes down to the things that are in your hands, you should also pray for help and the strength to actually do to them. But when the time for action arrives, it's entirely up to you. The more you articulate your goals in hitbodedut and break them down into small, do-able steps, the easier it will be to take the next step.

The Happiness Workshop

The ultimate goal of hitbodedut is to attain happiness! If you practice hitbodedut regularly, you will soon see the changes and improvements in your life. If you feel more relaxed, more optimistic and positive after a session of hitbodedut, it is the best sign that you are doing it right.

But don't expect release, insight, illumination and joy every time. Even the most assiduous practitioners of hitbodedut go through periods when they feel they are making little or no progress. Despite all their efforts, they find themselves tense, closed up, spiritually disconnected, frustrated, and unable or even unwilling to open their mouths to talk.

This is because hitbodedut is an active endeavour to elevate yourself spiritually. As soon as you face yourself as you really are and start grappling with yourself in order to take your life in hand, you will inevitably encounter powerful resisting forces. Some of these forces may be within yourself, others in the world around you. Often the resistance may become strongest when you are on the verge of a major breakthrough.

Even when you really want to talk to G-d, there may be times when you can think of nothing to say. At such moments simply say the word "G-d," or repeat the phrase, Ribono Shel Olam, "Master of the Universe." If you don't know who, what or where G-d is, or if you feel cut off spiritually, cry out: "Where are You?" If you can't speak, whisper. If you can't move your lips, say the words inside your heart.

There may be times when nothing works, no matter what you try. Sometimes things may be very bad. You may be assailed by negative thoughts. Life is full of pain and trouble. When we start examining ourselves, we may imagine that "nothing is sound from the soles of the feet to the top of the head – only wounds, bruises and festering sores" (Isaiah 1:6). We may feel that we are faced with insoluble problems on every side, while within ourselves all we see is pain, frustration anger, grief and contrition.

The essential work of hitbodedut is to dig and search beneath this surface negativity in order to uncover the redeeming sparks of good that exist everywhere, both in the external situations we face in our lives and within our own selves.

In the words of Rebbe Nachman: "You must seek out the good in yourself. Maybe when you start looking at yourself, it seems as if you have nothing good in you all. Even so, don't let yourself be discouraged. Search until you find even a modicum of good within yourself. Maybe when you start examining it, you feel it is full of blemishes. Even so, how is it possible that it does not contain even the tiniest amount of good? Search and search until you find some small good point in yourself that will give you new vitality and bring you to joy. And when you've found one good point, carry on searching until you find another... and another..."

"When you search for the positive points and gather them together, each good point becomes a 'note' in the melody of life. The music made by all these good points will bring life into your soul, and health and healing to your body. Then you will be able to pray and sing and give thanks to G-d!"

Doing it!

Hitbodedut may well turn out to be the single most important practice you adopt in order to bring your life to a higher level. Set regular times for hitbodedut. Work out the best time for you according to your schedule. Practice every day.

Sometimes people feel daunted by the idea of sitting down to meditate and pray for twenty minutes. If you find it hard to set a hitbodedut session, try it for just five minutes! Try it for even a single minute! Speak to G-d honestly for one minute! You'll find you can pour out many prayers even in as little as one minute!

At any time and place, you can always take a few moments for hitbodedut. It is always possible to snatch a little time to take a few deep breaths, offer some words of prayer, hum an inspiring melody, etc. You can do this even while washing dishes, standing in line at a checkout counter, or waiting to see a doctor, etc.

As a trial, take ten minutes for your first session of hitbodedut. You can practice hitbodedut right where you are at this very moment. Just decide that for the next ten minutes you are going to practice hitbodedut.

Spend the first five minutes sitting quietly, as discussed earlier. You might focus on your breathing or repeat a guide word such as "Shalom!" in order to settle your mind.

As you become calmer and clearer, you are ready for the second, more active phase of hitbodedut. Take a few moments to thank G-d for the good things in your life. Say the words out loud, or in a whisper. "Thank You for my life. Thank You for this. Thank You for that..."

Next, use guiding questions in order to become more aware of your thoughts and feelings. Ask yourself, "What am I thinking? What am I feeling? What is on my mind? What is really troubling me?" Ask these questions out loud or in a whisper.

Now start articulating your goals, needs and desires. Talk to G-d and to yourself about how you can attain them. You could spend five minutes or more on this active phase of hitbodedut. When you are ready to conclude, give thanks again for the good things and affirm your faith in G-d's ultimate goodness."

Written primarily for women, but of great potential value for all of us, **Inner Torah** by Miriam Millhauser describes a way of raising our consciousness of the Divine, through another form of meditative practice or introspective prayer that can be discovered within what she calls **The Inner Energy Body** and **The Inner Torah Scroll:**

"The physical body has an energy body within it. This energy body extends beyond the physical body, but for present purposes I want to focus on its inner dimension, which I call the inner energy body. Though we are often unaware of it in daily life, this inner body has as much reality as the physical body. It simply exists on a subtler, less dense plane. Yet it's unmistakable when contacted. It feels like a moving vibration. It flows in a current like water. It holds imprints of life experiences. And it is home to the self's Divine inner essence.

Why are we so far removed from the inner energy body? One explanation is that we are accustomed to focusing our attention outward. We use the world outside of us to anchor and stabilize ourselves. One sense or another is constantly providing a reference point in time and space through which we orient ourselves. We know where we are, and sometimes even who we are, from what we see, hear, taste, smell, and touch. That's why sensory deprivation can be so disorienting. It creates an environment where there is no outside stimuli to latch onto, throwing a person back on herself which, if she is not accustomed to being there, can be quite frightening.

So to move closer to our inner energy bodies we have to be prepared to shift focus from the world outside of us to the world within. To let go of our external frame of reference, however, necessitates that we have some other place to focus our attention, to feel held. The physical body is the next place that we encounter. It is the border between our inner realm and the outside world. By bringing attention to the physical body we begin to get a sense of being a container. The physical boundary of a body creates a space through which energy moves. Energy also moves through the parts of the body itself - the bones, muscles, ligaments, tissue, and cells.

Bringing attention to the level of the physical body itself is an accomplishment. Often we ignore it and experience ourselves as disembodied, aware of our thoughts but little else. To try to go from such a disembodied state directly to the inner energy body is hard. It is preferable to first bring awareness to the physical body, to focus on and bring attention to its different parts. In this way, we begin to cultivate an ability to sense, to become aware of ourselves on a bodily level. Initially we're likely to feel a slight tingling or warmth in areas where we put attention. Often even that much sensation is surprising if we've gone for a long time without conscious awareness of something so basic as, for example, our feet or hands. Essentially we are reacquainting ourselves with our primary home in the physical world. From there it is usually easier to develop awareness of the inner energy body.

The inner energy body is spacious and unbounded, yet contained. It invites stillness yet provides a gentle current of movement. There is a sense of floating free yet being solidly supported. Within it events and experiences of a lifetime come into sharper focus yet fade into the background of a bigger picture. Everything and its opposite, without contradiction, are held in a sea of energy waiting to be explored.

The Torah is G-d's communication to the Jewish people. Its content provides the guidance the Jewish nation needs to fulfill its mission. Stories are its primary medium. The scroll on which it is written is stored in a protective cabinet. We read it regularly, lovingly, and without end. We study it diligently, knowing that its stories are to be understood at increasingly deeper levels from surface to secret. We work to deepen our understanding. We review the same material repeatedly and often look to others to help us interpret correctly. This is the Torah with which we are all familiar, Torah from Sinai.

There is also an inner Torah. In my mind's eye, I see the scroll on which it is written in the body of every woman with whom I work. It contains the particular stories of her life, the particular guidance she needs to fulfill her mission, the communication that G-d is sending particularly to her. It sits protected in her torso. Regularly and lovingly she looks inside to read another portion. She reviews the same stories time and again, each time probing deeper into their meaning and gleaning yet another level of insight. Often she asks others for help.

The work of unearthing the secrets of her life circumstances is challenging. Like learning Torah, it requires meticulous attention to nuance and subtlety, willingness to review the same material repeatedly, openness to new interpretations. And, like learning Torah, it has no end, no limit to the depth that can be reached. The commitment required to persevere is significant. No life event falls outside the purview of scrutiny. For just as there is no extra letter or word in the Torah, nothing extraneous to G-d's message, so there is nothing extraneous in our lives. Everything that happens, no matter how seemingly insignificant, has a place in the bigger picture.

This is holy work. The women who have undertaken it are to be acknowledged and appreciated. Without reams of commentary they are tackling the raw material of their lives, trusting that through it G-d is communicating with them. To see this work as studying the inner Torah is important. It provides a context greater than the self for an effort that at times may feel overly self-focused. It avoids the discouragement and frustration that can easily arise when the same material is reviewed year after year, when the message is hard to comprehend or the lesson hard to implement. To be engaged in the process with total heart and might is itself worthy. For mastery of one's inner world is a necessary prerequisite to taking one's rightful place in creation. In time, as HaShem deems appropriate, understanding will come, the woman will move a step closer to her essence, and another aspect of HaShem's presence will be manifest in the world."

ASCENT for the SAKE of DESCENT

This is how Rabbi Avraham Sutton, the author of *Spiritual Technology*, writes about the dynamics of ascending into spiritual dimensions that are divinely encoded into the process of consciousness expansion:

"Picture yourself climbing higher and higher up a great mountain range. At each stage, you look back down and see greater expanses of the mountains, hills, towns, and valleys below. You can now see not only the township at the foot of the mountain, but the entire country in which you live within the greater context of which it is a part. In terms of ascending higher and higher up into the spiritual dimension, it means that the higher you go, each seemingly distinct universe or dimension through which you pass becomes revealed as a part within a greater whole, ad infinitum. The higher you go, the dimensions become more comprehensive and all-inclusive of all that is below them. The higher you go, the more you encounter complete and absolute **unity**. Such that, from those high plateaus, the **plurality** that you experienced below is now seen as an extension and an actualization of all that was always there within the Higher Unity in potential. What seemed, at a lower level, to be a distinct dimension, is revealed at the higher level to be merely a part within a greater whole.

Rebbe Nachman of Breslov — Endless Levels of Greater and More Encompassing Makifim (Transcendent Lights)

Even a *tzaddik* who has already done complete *teshuvah* must nevertheless continually do additional *teshuvah* for the level of *hasagah* (grasp, understanding) of HaShem's exaltedness that he was granted yesterday. For this is the nature of consciousness: Every moment opens up the possibility of a new *hasagah* that literally dwarfs what you understood yesterday. [Of course, you won't want to throw away or disparage what you grasped yesterday; on the contrary, without it, you wouldn't be able to stand where you are standing today.] This then is what we mean by having to constantly add *teshuvah* to *teshuvah*, for the level of *hasagah* of HaShem's exaltedness that you were granted yesterday is considered *megusham* (crude, rudimentary, insignificant) compared to the level you have been granted today (*Likutey Halakhot, Hilkhot Tefillin* 5:26).

Ratzo VaShov—Ascent for the Sake of Descent

Based on Ezekiel's famous description of the angels, "*Veha'chayot ratzo va'shov*—and the angels are constantly running and returning..." (Ezekiel 1:14), we know that all of creation is in constant motion. Running and returning. Dynamic oscillation. Ceaseless motion. Rebbe Nachman of Breslov understood how this applies to our inner lives as well. Instead of being passive in the face of life's ups and downs, he taught:[1]

You must know that every *yeridah* (descent) is *le'takhlit aliyah* (for the sake of a greater ascent). When a person falls from his level, he should know that this is from heaven. For the whole purpose of the apparent rejection [of heaven] is to draw him closer. The reason for the fall was/is to motivate him to make new efforts to come closer to G-d.

This is connected to another important teaching of Rebbe Nachman: "*Tzarikh lihiyot baki be'ratzo ve'baki be'shov*—you must be expert at running (i.e., going up, elevating, transcending); and you must be expert in returning (i.e., descending, coming back down)":[2]

[1] *Likutey Moharan* I, 261.
[2] *Meshivat Nefesh* 1, based on *Likutey Moharan* I, 6:4.

If you want to return to G-d, *tzarikh lihiyot baki ba'halakhah me'od*— you must be extremely expert/adept in the way you travel along the path towards G-d. Then, nothing in the world will bring you down or distance you from G-d as you ascend and [inevitably] descend. Rather, no matter what happens to you, you will be able to follow [King David's charge], "If I ascend to heaven, You are there. If I descend to the deepest hell, You are here!" (Psalms 139:8). Even in the deepest hell, you can come close to G-d [and become aware of His presence], for even there He is present, in the category of "If I descend to the deepest hell, You are here."[3]

Returning to G-d thus requires two types of expertise: *baki be'ratzo ve'baki be'shov* (expertise in running and expertise in returning). [It is thus written in the Zohar, "Happy is he who knows how to enter in peace and to depart in peace."[4]] This again is the meaning of "If I ascend to heaven, You are there. If I descend to the deepest hell, You are here."

"If I ascend to heaven" parallels "entering in peace" and "expert in running." "If I descend to the deepest hell" parallels "departing in peace" and "expert in returning."

Ratzo (running) represents going beyond yourself; bypassing and transcending your present limitations. In other words, *ratzo* (running) is *aliyah* (ascent); it is the experience of transcendence, the transcendental experience.

Shov (returning) basically involves coming back to normal consciousness after having been lifted up. Relative to the incredible "high" of the ascent, coming back to normal can sometimes seem like being in hell. The point is, however, to bring some of heaven into hell; to transform what could be experienced as a *yeridah* (descent), into the springboard for further *aliyot* (ascents). This is what Rebbe Nachman means about being *baki be'ratzo ve'baki be'shov*:

This means that, if, on the one hand, you are worthy of ascending to a certain level, whether great or small, you should not be content to stand still on this level. Rather, you must know and believe that you must advance further and further...On the other hand, even if you fall—even to what might feel like a bottomless pit—you should never give up hope in any way, come what may. Whatever happens, you must search out and entreat HaShem, and remain strong wherever you are and in whatever way you can. For He is with you even in the deepest pit, and from there you can bind yourself to Him, may He be blessed. This then is the meaning of, "If I descend to the deepest hell, You are here," the level of *baki bashov* (expert in returning).

There is no other way to return to G-d. You must attain expertise in these two ways. It certainly requires great skill and merit to know that at all times you must...yearn to reach the next higher level. Conversely, you must never let anything bring you down. You should never come to look down upon yourself. Only when you achieve expertise in these two ways will you be able to travel the path of return to G-d. G-d will then reach out to you to receive you.

[3] Notice the switch from *there* to *here*. Paradoxically, although HaShem is most hidden in the darkest hell, nevertheless, if we will it with all our might, we can break through the concealment to know Him in hell in a way that we never could have known Him in heaven.
[4] *Idra Zuta, Zohar Haazinu*, 3:292a.

The Up Down Dynamic

HaShem gives us a taste of heaven, and then all of a sudden, He casts us out. What's going on? HaShem isn't casting us out. Rather, He wants us to utilize what we've gotten in heaven. He wants us to take something back down with us into the darker parts of ourselves where there is hardly any light, where the light hardly ever penetrates, and internalize it there too. *Yeridah* (descent) and *shov* (returning) are thus not two different motions. On the contrary, HaShem lifts us up *davka* (precisely) so that we can now take this light that we have experienced and draw it down into every aspect of our being.

This is clearly not a one-time affair. The more we experience this dynamic the better we get at it, or at least the more we stand to gain from it. That is, the more we are able to go **up and in** in prayer, the more we are able to come back **down and out** with something precious and meaningful. The more we do this, the more we understand that this is what Torah, prophecy, and prayer are all about. Ultimately, this is what history is all about.

That is, going up and returning each time with more precious light is not only what an individual can and should be practicing all the time—for it is the essence dynamic behind all prayer and meditation—but it is the secret of why HaShem created the world, and us in it. It is the secret of why—after Avraham, Yitzchak, and Yaakov-Yisrael raised the consciousness of the world to recognize the existence of the Creator—the *bnei Yisrael* were forced to descend into the narrow straits and double binds of Mitzrayim.[5] It is the secret of why our souls have descended into this-world (the matrix). We have come here to transform the matrix of Mitzrayim into *Gan Eden*.

There is another reason why *aliyah* is so important: Beyond grasping, glimpsing, or understanding, which are all extremely important, there is merging. This merging involves a temporary loss of self, a *bitul ha'yesh* (nullification of self; ego-death), in order to be absorbed into the **One**. Because this is beyond relationship, beyond I-Thou, it sounds frightening. But again, we are promised that every *ratzo* is followed by a *shov*. Here, *shov* is not only a return to normalcy, but an internalization of the experience of oneness to such an extent that we become transformed.

This transformation of the individual consciousness is part of the great transformation of consciousness on this planet that will culminate in "I [HaShem] will pour forth My prophetic spirit on all flesh..." (Joel 3:1), and "The earth will be filled with the consciousness of HaShem as the waters cover the sea" (Isaiah 11:9).

In the meantime, the purpose of every *shov* (return) after a *ratzo* (running) is to draw the light of heaven down into the earth plane, to amplify the consciousness of G-d in the world. In this way, the coarseness of earth becomes refined and irradiated with divine light. This is the meaning of what we pray for in so many of our prayers:

"*Galei kevod malkhut'kha alenu bim'hera be'yameinu*—reveal the glory of Your kingdom upon us, soon, in our days!"[6] "*Tair eretz mi'kevodekha*—irradiate the earth-plane with Your glory."[7] "*Barukh ha'meir la'olam kulo bi'khvodo*—blessed is He who irradiates the entire world with His glory."[8]

We then realize what it means that the *ratzo va'shov* (running and returning) of the angels is a metaphor for the *ratzo va'shov* of creation: It means that **all comes from the Creator** and **all returns**. This becomes so clear to us (in a state of *aliyah-ratzo*) that we realize that this is happening all the time. Yes, creation is constantly being created, and it is also constantly returning to its source. This is happening at such a high frequency and at such a depth that we are completely unaware of it."

[5] We read in the *Haggadah*, "*Vayered Mitzraima* (but he [Yaakov] descended to Egypt), *anoos al pi hadibur* (compelled by divine decree)."
[6] *Mussaf Shalosh Regalim.*
[7] *Yedid Nefesh.*
[8] *Kriat Shma al HaMitah.*

THE BREATH OF LIFE

"It is clear from all our traditions that we define G-d primarily as the Creator of all things. We find this in the very opening verse of the Torah, which says, 'In the beginning, G-d created the heaven and the earth.' This is a statement about creation, but it also tells us that G-d is the Creator.

When we speak of G-d as Creator of 'heaven and earth', we are not just speaking of the visible world. G-d's creation includes every possible thing that exists. The Bible clearly tells us that there is absolutely nothing that is outside the domain of G-d's creation, as He told His prophet, 'I am G-d, I make all things' (Isaiah 44:24).

We may be able to conceive of other universes. There may be worlds beyond our imagination. All of them, however, ultimately emanate from G-d. This is what the Psalmist meant when he said, 'Your dominion is a kingdom of all worlds' (Psalms 145:13).

There are many things that are difficult to imagine as emanating from G-d. For example, there is so much evil in the world, and one may be tempted to think of it as coming from a separate power, independent of G-d. Nothing could be further from the truth; everything ultimately comes from G-d. If we understand G-d's purpose in creation, we understand why evil must exist. But it is most important to realize that there is no power independent of G-d's creation. He therefore told His prophet, 'I form light and create darkness, I make peace and create evil, I am G-d. I do all these things' (Isaiah 45:7).

The very word 'create' – *Bara* in Hebrew – implies creating something out of nothing. Otherwise, we use the word 'make' or 'form'. When we say that G-d created the universe, we mean that He created it absolutely *ex nihilo* – out of nothing. This is alluded to in the verse, 'He hangs the world upon nothingness' (Job 26:7).

The *Midrash* tells us that a philosopher once remarked to Rabban Gamliel, 'Your G-d is a wonderful artist, but He had fine materials to work with. When He made the world, He fashioned it out of waste and desolation, darkness, wind, water and depths.' Rabban Gamliel replied, 'Your words are mere wind! All of these things were also created by G-d.'

The act of creation involved absolutely no effort on the part of G-d. When the Torah says that He 'rested' on the seventh day, it does not mean that He rested because He was weary or tired after six days of hard work. Rather it means that G-d stopped creating after six days, since the world was completed with the creation of man. The act of creation, however, involved absolutely no effort on the part of G-d, as the prophet Isaiah taught, 'Do you not know? Have you not heard? The Eternal, the everlasting G-d, Creator of the wide world, grows neither weary nor faint' (Isaiah 40:28).

This is because G-d is absolutely infinite. To an infinite Being, the entire universe is like nothing, and therefore, its creation involves no effort. The Bible thus says, 'Everything on earth is like nothing to Him. He does as He wills with the host of heaven and the hordes of the earth' (Daniel 4:32). Every possible thing, even the creation of the universe, is infinitely easy for an infinite G-d.

In order to emphasize the fact that G-d's creation involves no effort, the Torah speaks of it as done with words. Each act of creation begins with the expression, 'And G-d said.' The Psalmist explicitly states, 'With the word of G-d were the heavens made, with the breath of His mouth, all their host … For He spoke and it was, He commanded, and it stood' (Psalms 33:6,9). The *Midrash* comments of this: 'Not with work nor effort did G-d create the universe, but with a mere word.'

In expressing the absence of effort in the act of creation, our sages teach us that it did not even involve a word, but a mere letter of the alphabet. This furthermore was not just any letter, but the one letter that is most easily pronounced. They teach us that the world was created by the letter *Heh*, the Hebrew equivalent of 'H'. Pronouncing this letter involves no more effort than the slightest breath. With such a small effort G-d created the universe.

When we say that the world was created with G-d's word, we are, of course, using a metaphor. G-d did not actually speak in a physical sense. He merely willed the existence of all things. His very wisdom and knowledge implied creation. When the Torah says that He spoke, it merely does so to tell us that creation was a willful act. In actuality, however, G-d's creation came about as a direct result of His wisdom and knowledge. The Prophet said, 'He made the earth with His power, founded the world with His wisdom, and unfurled the skies with His understanding' (Jeremiah 10:12)."

Extracts from G-D by Rabbi Aryeh Kaplan

SENSE OF SMELL AND MASHIACH

by Efrat Rivka Sari

Sense of Smell from Creation

וַיִּיצֶר יי אֱלֹקִים אֶת־הָאָדָם עָפָר מִן־הָאֲדָמָה וַיִּפַּח בְּאַפָּיו נִשְׁמַת חַיִּים וַיְהִי הָאָדָם לְנֶפֶשׁ חַיָּה:

"HaShem Elokim formed man from the dust of the ground, and breathed into his nostrils the breath of life; and man became a living soul."

(Genesis 2:7)

Where does the Breath of Life enter? Into the nostrils! In Lamentations, it reveals the secret of the Breath of Life:

רוּחַ אַפֵּינוּ מְשִׁיחַ יי

"The breath of our nostrils, the Messiah of HaShem, was taken in their pits; of whom we said, Under his shadow we shall live among the nations."

(Lamentations 4:20)

The breath of our nostrils is the Messiah! The Mashiach is the one who resurrects the dead. Chaim Kramer, of the Breslov Research Institute writes,

"Mashiach is represented by the "nose," our source of life and breath. . . As long as we breathe the breath of hope – the breath of prayer and reliance upon G-d – there is hope that Mashiach will come and fully purify our lives. The verse states (Lamentations 4:2), "The breath of our nostrils [is] the Mashiach of G-d."

118

Amazingly, the breath breathed into Adam occurred on Rosh HaShanah, the day of Resurrection:

"Man becomes a living, sentient being when G-d breathes His breath into him, transforming him from physical matter into a living hybrid of the physical and spiritual. When we blow the shofar on the day of Man's creation, it serves as a memorial to that first breath, the divine breath of life blown at the dawn of Creation, on Rosh HaShanah."

R. Ari Kahn: The Sound of the Shofar

Chaim Kramer then makes an astonishing statement:

"...just as breathing sustains each person, whether one is conscious of it or not, so too, Mashiach, the world's ultimate rectification, has sustained the world from its inception, whether we are conscious of it or not."

Just as prayer links to the incense, Kramer notes,

"Mashiach will "breathe the fear of G-d," since his soul is rooted in the place of breathing, the nose. And this "nose," the source of life of the Mashiach, alludes to prayer. Rebbe Nachman thus taught: Mashiach's main weapon is prayer..." Thus prayer is represented by the nose. And the nose is breathing, life itself."

He continues,

"...[Mashiach's] "breathing" will have a very positive effect upon mankind. . . The breath that Mashiach will breathe will emanate from the Torah and its 613 mitzvot. This is "The spirit of G-d [that] hovered over the waters." The spirit is Mashiach and the waters are the Torah. Mashiach's spirit is embedded in the Torah and he will draw his breath, the awe of G-d, from it. With this spirit, he will be able to "breathe into others" filing them with an awe and respect for G-d."

HAVDALAH

At the end of Shabbat, there is a service called הַבְדָּלָה Havdalah, which means "separation". It sets the Shabbat apart from the ordinary days of the week. A braided Candle, a Kiddush Cup, and a box of Spices, called b'samim in Hebrew.

Our Rabbis have made an interesting observation about Havdalah, noting that, "All the senses are used in blessing the wine, the light of a special candle and smelling spices."

As we see the light

Feel the heat,

Taste the wine,

And smell the spices,

We hear the blessing...

ברוך אתה יי אלוקינו מלך העולם בורא מיני בשמים

"Barukh ata HaShem Elokeinu melekh ha-olam, borei minei b'samim."

"Blessed are you, HaShem our G-d, King of the Universe, who creates the species of fragrances."

Growing up, my grandmother taught me a saying, "Believe nothing of what you hear, and only half of what you see."

The prophet Isaiah,

"A shoot will come out of the stock of Jesse, and a branch out of his roots will bear fruit. The Spirit of HaShem will rest on him: the spirit of wisdom and understanding, the spirit of counsel and might, the spirit of knowledge and of the fear of the Eternal. His delight (וַהֲרִיחוֹ) will be in the fear of HaShem. He will not judge by the sight of his eyes, neither decide by the hearing of his ears…"

(Isaiah 11:1-3)

Rabbi Nachman of Breslov points out various sources in which the Mashiach is associated with the sense of smell. Yirmiyahu refers to the Mashiach as the "breath of our noses" (Eichah 4:24). And the word "Mashiach" itself means literally "anointed", referring to the fragrant oil used to anoint the kings of Israel. So one sign of the true Mashiach is that he will be able to "smell and judge" – to determine the guilt and innocence of defendants by directly sensing their inner nature (Sanhedrin 93b).

Mashiach is above what is seen and what is heard. So often we may judge a person by their personal appearance or what family they are from. Perhaps we are easily swayed by rumors or what is heard. Ruach [spirit] and rei'ach [scent] have amazing similarities. There is a mysterious interplay between the two.

Mashiach can discern the scent of the spirit of an individual. Each person has a unique scent to their being. A dog can tell its master just by the scent. Just as each one has a different scent so also do they have a different spirit. Mashiach has G-d-given senses that are above Halachah and our ability to understand.

The term Yericho (Jericho) derives from the word rei'ach (smell), and alludes to Mashiach of whom it is said "veharicho b'yirat HaShem – in the fear of G-d..." (Isaiah 11:3): that is, Mashiach is called "mari'ach veda'in – he is able to judge a person by merely 'smelling' him" (Sanhedrin 93b).

Soon we will be able to greet the Mashiach, who will instantly and perfectly perceive the spiritual aspect of everything, and transmit his knowledge to mankind. This is one reason why we make a special point of a blessing on spices as Shabbat goes out (Havdalah ceremony). Then we have a heightened expectation of greeting Eliyahu who will herald the arrival of Mashiach (Likutei Halakhot, Laws of Blessings on Smell).

The verse "All the souls shall praise G-d" (Tehillim 150:6) teaches us that there is a praise of G-d which belongs to the soul alone. The Talmud asks, "What is it that provides enjoyment for the soul but not for the body? Fragrance" (Berakhot 43b).

At the simplest level, the statement that smell benefits the soul and not the body means that smell does not fulfill any bodily need and does not become part of the body – unlike food and drink. For this reason, we could think that it is not a real or substantial enjoyment, and does not require a blessing. That is why a Biblical source (or hint) for the obligation is required.

This means that the sense of smell has the ability to create a certain response in our brain prior to our logical consideration. Often this response comes in the form of a memory, or a strong emotional response to a certain aroma. HaShem made use of His beautiful design to engage Klal Yisroel in Tefillah (prayer) and worship through the sense of smell.

We must also understand that we must care for our bodies. "It is meritorious to anoint our bodies for healing because our bodies are a miniature image of the Holy Temple". If we do not take care of our body's Temple then we have a hint in Leviticus 26:31 "And I will... bring your sanctuaries unto desolation, and I will not smell the savor of your sweet odors."

HaShem commands Moshe to use a blend of essential oils to make what would be called "Holy Anointing Oil." This blend of oils was used to anoint almost every holy vessel in the Tabernacle, and it was used to anoint priests. HaShem was very specific that it was not to be used on any person, other than a priest; and, it was not to be used for common purposes. But that does not mean we cannot use the plant essences of G-d's creation to anoint our bodies to be healed so that we may live a life to fill the world with His Torah and perform His Mitzvot.

Every time Klal Yisroel gathered to worship, the aroma of Holy Ketoret and the Holy anointing oil would fill the people gathering. HaShem had a very specific purpose in doing this. He was teaching the nation of Israel that this aroma was the aroma of worship. This concept is a difficult one for us to grasp. But, the sense of smell has a very powerful effect on the brain. Of the five senses, the sense of smell is the only one that is processed through the emotional part of the brain before it goes through the logical part of the brain.

This Holy aroma, as much as sacrifices, laws, and rituals, was a part of Jewish Temple corporate worship. It was the part of our worship that engaged the sense of smell. Because the scent passed through the emotional seat of the brain, the activities of worship were reinforced! The ability to experience the sense of smell is an amazing blessing from G-d. The fact that He can use our sense of smell to draw us nearer to Him is yet another example of His amazing love poured out on us like oil of sweet Myrrh and Frankincense.

THE KETORET

The Ketoret, or Incense, was a powerful aromatic aspect of the Temple service. It must have had a wonderful scent, as there is an explicit command in the Torah not to use it for perfume.

"The incense which you shall make, according to its composition you shall not make for yourselves: it shall be to you holy for HaShem. Whoever shall make any like that, to smell of it, he shall be cut off from his people."

(Exodus 30:37-38)

Consisting of eleven ingredients, its scent was extremely powerful according to ancient accounts,

"The goats in Jericho used to sneeze because of the odor of the incense. The women in Jericho did not have to perfume themselves, because of the odor of the incense. The bride in Jerusalem did not have to perfume herself because of the odor of the incense."

(Yoma 39b, Talmud)

All of Jerusalem was a fragrant aroma to HaShem affecting the entire atmosphere. Amazingly, the Torah compares the incense to prayer, "Let my prayer be set before you like ketoret (incense), the lifting up of my hands like the evening sacrifice."

(Psalms 141:2)

THE NOSE KNOWS

It is very much worth noting that in the Genesis account of Adam's creation, it is said that G-d 'breathed into his nostrils the breath of life'–not into his body, mouth, or lungs, but the nose–'and man became a living soul' (Genesis 2:7). 'Nostrils…living soul' indicates that breath awareness in the nostril makes us conscious–aware of spirit. Three more times in Genesis (6:17; 7:15, 22) we find the expression 'breath of life', and in each instance breath is equated with life itself. In seven further instances in the Torah, the life principle is referred to, not just as the breath, but as the breath in the nostrils (Genesis 7:22; II Samuel 22:16; Job 4:9; 27:3; Psalms 18:16; Isaiah 2:22; Lamentations 4:20). This cannot be without significance. This verse, however, tells us more.

First, we learn that the breath comes directly from G-d, second, that through it 'man became a living soul'–it is the breath that makes the psychic part of our makeup to live, just as it makes the body live. From this it becomes evident that the breath and spirit are the same; that the breath of life is the spirit of life–and ultimately is Divinity Itself. 'The Spirit of G-d has made me, and the breath of the Almighty has given me life' (Job 33:4). Meditation on the breath, then, is a way of directly meditating on G-d–'the G-d in whose hand your breath is' (Daniel 5:23).

G-d is 'He that gives breath unto the people upon [the Earth], and spirit to them that walk therein' (Isaiah 42:5). Just as the breath of G-d is the Spirit of G-d, so also, since we are made in His image and likeness (Genesis 1:26), our breath, one with our spirit, is our true nature and self. 'Thus says the Eternal G-d unto these bones; Behold, I will cause breath to enter into you, and you shall live. And I will lay sinews upon you, and will bring up flesh upon you, and cover you with skin, and put breath in you, and you shall live....Thus says the Eternal G-d; Come from the four winds, O breath, and breathe upon these slain, that they may live....So I prophesied as He commanded me, and the breath came into them, and they lived' (Ezekiel 37:5, 6, 9, 10). In Lamentations 4:20 we see that Mashiach is called 'the breath of our nostrils'.

The breath of G-d is His creative power; and all things were made by it. That power is *Ruach HaKodesh* (the Holy Spirit). It is G-d 'in whose hand is the soul of every living thing, and the breath of all mankind' (Job 12:10). Even more, the breath of G-d is the breath of mankind: 'All the while my breath is in me, and the spirit of G-d is in my nostrils' (Job 27:3).

Health and Breath

The breath being the principle of life, it is also has a power of healing. This is perceived right away by those who give adequate time to meditating on their breath. It is also the condition of the breath that produces disease and death. 'My breath is corrupt, my days are extinct, the graves are ready for me' (Job 17:1). The breath is not only the means by which life enters into us–as stated in the first verse considered above– it is also the means by which we depart from this world into another, for Job says: 'By the breath of his mouth shall he go away' (Job 15:30). Cultivation of the breath is cultivation of life and health.

The Silence

Silent awareness is the prime characteristic and purpose of breathing meditation. Throughout the Torah, silence and quiescence are set forth as essential for perceiving our Neshamah (Spirit). 'Their strength is to sit still' (Isaiah 30:7). 'Be aware and be quiet' (Isaiah 7:4). 'Be silent, all flesh, before the Eternal' (Zechariah 2:13). 'Then are they glad because they became quiet; so He brings them unto their desired haven' (Psalms 107:30).

This silence has a practical effect. 'Stand still, and see the salvation of the Eternal' (Exodus 14:13). 'Moses said unto them: Stand still, and I will hear what the Eternal will command concerning you' (Numbers 9:8). Also Samuel: 'Stand still a while, that I may show you the word of G-d' (I Samuel 9:27). Again, 'You shall not need to fight in this battle: set yourselves, stand still, and see the salvation of the Eternal with you' (II Chronicles 20:17).

Through Isaiah the Eternal has said: 'Keep silence before Me, and let the people renew their strength' (Isaiah 41:1). 'They that wait upon the Eternal in silent awareness shall renew their strength; they shall mount up with wings as eagles; they shall run, and not be weary; and they shall walk, and not faint' (Isaiah 40:31). It is indeed true that 'The Eternal is good unto them that wait for him, to the soul that seeks him. It is good that a man should both hope and quietly wait for the salvation of the Eternal…let him sit alone and keep silence' (Lamentations 3:25, 26, 28).

'Therefore the prudent shall keep silence in that time' (Amos 5:13). 'Stand still, and consider the wondrous works of G-d' (Job 37:14). 'Commune with your own heart, and be still' (Psalms 4:4). 'Rest in the Eternal, and wait patiently for Him' (Psalms 37:7). 'Be still, and know that I am G-d' (Psalms 46:10). 'The Eternal is in His holy Temple: let all the earth keep silence before Him' (Habakkuk 2:20). 'Be silent, all flesh, before the Eternal: for He is raised up out of His holy habitation' (Zechariah 2:13).

'There is a path which no fowl knows, and which the vulture's eye hath not seen' (Job 28:7). Speaking of that time of profound tranquility, David sang: 'He leads me beside the still waters' (Psalms 23:2).

The Voice in the Silence

'And Elijah arose, and went unto Horeb the mount of G-d. And he came thither unto a cave, and lodged there; and, behold, the word of the Eternal came to him, and He said unto him...Go forth, and stand upon the mount before the Eternal. And, behold, the Eternal passed by, and a great and strong wind rent the mountains, and brake in pieces the rocks before the Eternal; but the Eternal was not in the wind: and after the wind an earthquake; but the Eternal was not in the earthquake: And after the earthquake a fire; but the Eternal was not in the fire: and after the fire *a still small voice*. And it was so, when Elijah heard it, that he wrapped his face in his mantle, and went out, and stood in the entrance of the cave. And, behold, there came a voice unto him' (I Kings 19:8-13).

"My Heart Wakes"

David counsels us: 'Commune with your own heart upon your bed, and be still' (Psalms 4:4). 'When the sun was going down, a deep sleep fell upon Abram' (Genesis 15:12). It is of this waking sleep that David further sang: 'He gives to His beloved in sleep' (Psalms 127:2). 'As for me, I will behold thy face in righteousness: I shall be satisfied when I awake with Your likeness' (Psalms 17:15). 'When I awake, I am still with You' (Psalms 139:18). Speaking of that state, Jeremiah said this: 'Upon this I awoke, and beheld; and my sleep was sweet unto me' (Jeremiah 31:26). In the sweet sleep of inner awareness we truly awake and see. As David says, 'I laid me down and slept; [yet] I awoke' (Psalms 3:5). Solomon also speaks of this, 'I sleep, but my heart wakes'

(Song of Songs 5:2). Both Daniel and Zechariah speak of their inmost experiences as being 'asleep' (Daniel 8:18, 10:9; Zechariah 4:1).

This waking sleep is also referred to as 'rest' in the Torah. 'My flesh also shall rest in hope' (Psalms 16:9). 'Return unto your rest, O my soul' (Psalms 116:7). The prophets other than David also spoke of this mystic experience. 'The whole earth is at rest, and is quiet' (Isaiah 14:7). 'This is the rest wherewith you may cause the weary to rest; and this is the refreshing' (Isaiah 28:12).

The Breath as a Pathway to G-d

"The goal of meditation, especially as described by the Kabbalistic masters, is to attain enlightenment. In Hebrew, the word most often used to describe such enlightenment is *Ruach HaKodesh*, which can literally be translated as 'Holy Spirit.' It is this term that is consistently used by all Hebrew writers.

....As we have seen, Rabbi Abraham Maimonides explains that the 'pure heart' for which King David prayed (Psalms 51:12-14) refers to a heart and mind cleansed of all external thoughts through intense meditation.
The level of enlightenment implied by *Ruach HaKodesh* involves a clarity of understanding, an enhancement of perception, an awareness of the spiritual.

While in its lowest state, *Ruach HaKodesh* consists of general enlightenment and perception, in its higher, true states, *Ruach HaKodesh* provides the individual with clear, unequivocal perception, where he can actually receive information that is not otherwise available.

Although G-d's influence constantly permeates man's being, like the air around us, it is not usually detected. Air can only be felt when it is in motion, when we sense it as a wind *(Ruach)*. Similarly, G-d's spirit can only be detected when it moves in us [as the breath], and it is for this reason that such spirit is also called *Ruach*, the same word as for wind.

This is also evident from the etymology of the word *Ruach*. This word is closely related to the Hebrew word *Ore'ach*, meaning a 'visitor' or 'guest,' as well as the word *Orach* meaning path."

Rabbi Aryeh Kaplan from *Meditation and the Bible*

As Rabbi Yitzchak Ginsburgh explains: "The word for 'delight' (v'haricho) has the same root as the word for 'smell' (rayach). The Sages interpretation of this is of the ability of Mashiach to judge through the sense of smell. According to tradition, the four senses of sight, hearing, taste and touch were all blemished due to their participation in the sin of eating from the tree of knowledge of good and evil in the Garden of Eden. Only the sense of smell does not appear in the verses describing the sin, thus retaining its original pristine state. The common expressions 'something doesn't smell right' and 'this stinks' used to illustrate situations that feel intuitively wrong, allude to the association between smell and judgment. Smell is connected to intuition, both of which emanate from a superconscious level above logic and reason."

WHERE HEAVEN TOUCHES EARTH

Rabbi Avraham Sutton vividly shines a light here on the many teachings by spiritual giants that point to the truth that the Torah's ultimate purpose is to allow us to experience G-d:

"Kabbalah (starting with the prophets, and then continuing on in the Zohar and the Midrashim, and then in the Ari) talks a lot about how spiritual reality impacts on physical reality. It does this by using physical terms to describe spiritual realities. When understood properly, we see that they did this in order to inform us that **physicality does not exist separately and apart from the spiritual. Physical reality is rather an extension and outward manifestation of a higher level of existence that preceded it. Physical reality is an outer *levush* (garment) that covers the spirit. Once this profound truth is understood, it is possible to proceed to the next stage: We are to turn our sights upward, to envision and experience (to the extent possible) the spiritual reality of our own soul *mufshat* (divested, unclothed) of physicality.**

The first stage of Kabbalah is called *hit'labshut*, clothing one thing in another, the interpenetration and indwelling of the spiritual in the physical. **Only after we see through the *levush* of this outer world (*ohr* with an ayin - skin) --- and at least intuit that there is a whole world of *ohr with an aleph* (light) behind it --- only then do we then reverse the order to practice *hafshatah* (divestment).**

Kabbalah is very explicit about all this. **Nothing down here just exists. Everything has its root above.** The Kabbalah of the Ari is an advanced system for not only understanding but experiencing the higher energy levels that precede our world. **The way to do this is to refine and sharpen our spiritual eyesight, to penetrate beneath the façade of physical reality. Living down here in a world of *ohr* with an *ayin*, the** concept of soul is abstract. We thus need to work backwards from below to understand how things were before *ohr* with an *aleph* coalesced into *ohr* with an *ayin*. The process of working up from below, from concrete to abstract, is called *hafshatah*. In Hebrew, *mufshat* (abstract) comes from skinning an animal and also removing/divesting a garment ("*pashateti et kutonti*," Song of Songs 5:3). *Hafshatah* allows us to see through the outer form of something and access its *penimiyut* (inner essence). From the perspective of the physical world, *hafshatah* is abstract. From the perspective of the *elyon* (the higher spiritual reality that precedes and is the source of our world) *hafshatah* is return to essence, divesting of lower concrete form. Like when the soul is released from being constricted in the body, or when the light of the sun shines unhampered.

This was what Yaakov Avinu meant when he said, "*Akhen yesh YKVK bamakom hazeh*—truly HaShem is in this **place**, but I did not know it!" For it was there in that amazing place where heaven touches earth that Yaakov transcended earthly life to receive the heavenly vision of his life. There, at the very spot of the Holy of Holies, he entered the holy of holies of his own being. There he met G-d and he knew that, in that place which is not a place, because it transcends place as we know it, **in that place, there is no separate existence**. This is where he realized "*ein od mi'levado*—there is nothing but G-d" (Deuteronomy 4:39). **There is only HaShem**

The Torah is All About Directly Experiencing G-d
Nefesh HaChayim 1:5 (*hagahah hi ikar ha'adam*)

The body is thus like a shoe relative to [the entire stature of] the soul. Just as only the foot, which is the lowest extremity of the body, can fit into a shoe, so also may only the lowest extremity of the soul fit into the body. For the body is called "the extremities of the feet [of the soul]" within which the soul becomes clothed. The higher aspects of the soul remain outside and above the body, and rise up above it to the highest spiritual dimension. In all this, the role of the body is that of a curtain which prevents an overabundance of the soul's light and intensity from illuminating the physical world. This is alluded to in HaShem's statement to Moshe, when he stood at the burning bush, "Remove your

133

shoes from your feet, for the place upon which you are standing is holy ground" (Exodus 3:5). [In addition to the plain meaning of this statement (i.e., the actual removal of the shoes),] HaShem was indicating to Moshe that he must divest his soul of its physical sheath [in order to be able to withstand the powerful spiritual light that He wished to bestow on him at that time].

Prayer—The Virtual Temple of the Soul

Yaakov Avinu meant when he said, "*Akhen yesh YKVK bamakom hazeh*—truly HaShem is in this **place**, but I did not know it!" For it was there in that amazing place where heaven touches earth that Yaakov transcended earthly life to receive the heavenly vision of his life. There, at the very spot of the Holy of Holies, he entered the holy of holies of his own being. There he met G-d and he knew that, in that place which is not a place, because it transcends place as we know it, **in that place, there is no separate existence**. This is where he realized "*ein od mi'levado*—there is nothing but G-d" (Deuteronomy 4:39). **There is only HaShem**.

Put yourself in Yaakov's place. He is in a deep meditative trance. He has done everything that his father, grandfather, and teachers taught him in order to enter the prophetic state. He has quieted his mind and entered deeply within in order to ascend to the top of the ladder of his soul. He prepares for this by starting at the base of his spine, the human counterpart of the *Evven Shetiyah* sunk deeply into the earth. Slowly, he begins raising his consciousness—the intense focus of his awareness— up the eighteen vertebrae of the ladder of his spine. At the top of his spine, he stops to focus and waits to be allowed to enter the holy of holies of his brain stem. "*Akhen yesh HaShem bamakom hazeh*—truly HaShem is in this place." He enters and moves up into the middle brain, the membrane between the tablets of the covenant (the right and left hemispheres of his brain), all the way to the top, to the space between the *keruvim*.

HaShem now opens something in Yaakov's brain. It is as if the two hemispheres of his brain unfurl and open like the wings of the *keruvim*. And in that space that is beyond space, he knew: "*Mah nora hamakom hazeh*—how awesome is this **place**. This is none other than *Beit Elokim* (G-d's Temple on earth)! This is the gate to heaven." Here, the word *makom* no longer refers to a place in which HaShem dwells. Here is where Yaakov breaks through the illusion of space-time and realizes that HaShem Himself is the *Makom* of the universe. Most importantly for us, it is this revelation that lifts Yaakov up and transforms him into one of the greatest human beings to have ever walked this earth. This is why the rabbis skipped over the literal meaning of the word *makom* (place), and saw it rather as a direct reference to the fact that HaShem is the place of the world.

The holy of holies experience is a state of consciousness called *devekut* wherein whatever physical, emotional, mental, and/or spiritual blocks that are preventing us from realizing that we are always standing in HaShem's presence dissolve. Seen from this holy-of-holies perspective, our normal experience of the world is really a necessary illusion that HaShem created so that we could think, feel, and act as if we exist separately from Him. Here in the holy of holies, the illusion disappears and we realize that we are always *lifney HaShem*—in HaShem's presence. Again, our *avodah* (inner work), after having entered *lifnay ve'lifnim*, is to return with as much of that higher awareness as possible into all the outer courtyards of our life.

Most important, once we reach the top of the ladder and the mountain, and enter into the holy of holies, it is essential to stop all extraneous speech and thought. Here, in order to hear the G-dly voice, we need to **be in silence**. For this is the place where heaven touches earth, where we transcend our earthly life to **receive** the heavenly vision of our life. Beyond anything, prayer is about how to meet G-d in that holy of holies and to know that, in that place, which is not a place, because it transcends place as we know it, **in that place, there is no separate existence**. This is where we realize "*ein od mi'levado*—there is nothing but G-d" (Deuteronomy 4:39). **There is only HaShem**. In this inner place we realize that our little "i" is an extension of the Great "I". We nullify our existence to the Source of existence, in order to receive much greater and truer existence in return.

This is the core experience toward which all Jewish prayer and meditation aims. The work is then to internalize this experience and take it with us as we walk back *down* and *out* into the outer courtyards of our life.

Inwardness, how to get to and enter into an inner place within where we connect directly with Source. This inner place is behind the scenes of our lives. It is always there. It is hidden from us but it is nevertheless always there. Once we have a taste of what that sacred inner place is like, we will want to return. We will want to make this place the center from which we live our lives. We mentioned Moshe Rabbeinu's prophetic experience at the burning bush, which was his first experience of this inner place. I urge you to discover your own burning bush experience and to make it a mainstay of your life. Yaakov Avinu's first real-life experience of this place was after he left the yeshivah of Shem and Evver, and was on his way to Charan to marry. *"Vayifga bamakom*—he hit upon the **place**."

One more point before I go on. HaShem has brought our souls down to earth at a very crucial time on the planet. It is important for us to register this, that what is going on inside us, what is going on around us globally, and what is going on around us cosmically and spiritually — — it is all being choreographed from above. As we mentioned, we are now in a culmination stage of history, a powerful end-time scenario unfolding before our eyes. Events much bigger than us unfolding before our eyes. Whether we understand it or not is not important. The fact is that He is the source for all that is going on. He is setting up the scenes. We are the actors. Our job is to establish an inner connection with the Him in the midst of all this. He wants us to be Avrahams and Sarahs, Yaakovs and Leahs and Rachels. He wants us to be Yosephs and Yehudahs and Moshes. He wants us to be Miriams and Yocheveds, Ruths and Naomis. He wants us to be Shmuels and Davids and Shlomos. He wants to be Mattityahus and Yehudits and Mordechais and Esthers. He wants us to connect our soul with theirs, to take on the work that they began, to be extensions of their great souls. Actually we already are, but until now it's been unconscious. Now we have to say, *"Hineini!* Here we are! We are ready HaShem! We only want to serve You!" The only way to do this is to establish this deep inner connection with Him in the inner sanctum of our soul. This is what is called for. This is what we are trying to do here, nothing less.

We need to be able to connect with deeper and deeper levels of our own being, in order to get to and enter an inner place within where we connect directly with Source. This inner place is always there. It is hidden but nevertheless always there. This is what Torah/Kabbalah reveals to us. We usually look at the world from the *outside-in* and from the *bottom-up*. We see a world of multiplicity, of fragmentation and divisions, and we conjecture or even come to believe that there is something, some essential unity, that precedes and is the source of all this. The Torah comes and tells us, don't strain. You don't have to believe anything. You rather have to remove what is preventing you from knowing that *HaShem Elokekhem emet*, the Infinite One is one and only. He/It is Reality with a capital R. *Ein od mi'levado*—on the inside-inside level, nothing else exists but Him."

Or Makif - The Love of the Creator

In *Ten Luminous Emanations*, revealing the teachings of Rabbi Yitzchak Luria (the Ari), Rabbi Yehudah Ashlag discusses the mysteries of life, the Creator and the cosmos. Explaining how Rav Ashlag describes the concept of Surrounding Light (Or Makif) that the Ari speaks about, Michael Berg writes the following:

"We learn from Rav Ashlag in *Ten Luminous Emanations* that the way we receive the Light of the Creator in our world is very different than the way it was in the Endless World. In the Endless World, the Light of the Creator shined whether or not we deserved it - the Creator gave and we received. Our world was then created because we wanted the opportunity to perfect ourselves through earning the Light. In our reality, we earn the Light through transforming our selfish Desire to Receive for the Self Alone into a Desire to Receive for the sake of giving pleasure to the Creator.

After the Creation, there is now a barrier between us and the Light. This barrier is the basis of any lack of fulfillment we have in our lives. We usually think of a barrier as something stopping us from getting what we want. But Rav Ashlag teaches us that the barrier is actually our selfish

Desire, and that barrier is only removed to the degree that we no longer want for ourselves. The barrier is an exact measurement of how much we Desire to Receive for the Self Alone. The more selfish our Desire, the stronger that barrier. The only Light that can come into our lives is Light that we receive solely with the intention to give pleasure to the Creator.

As we study *Ten Luminous Emanations* and begin to understand these concepts, Rav Ashlag introduces us to an incredible exception to the rule – the concept of *Or Makif*, or "Surrounding Light." This is Light that we have not earned. There are two types of *Or Makif*. The first is our potential – the Light that we can receive if we fully transform our Desire. For instance, if I enjoy receiving only for the sake of giving pleasure to the Creator 10% of the time, I only receive 10% of the Light, and the other 90% shines as *Or Makif*.

The second form of *Or Makif* is an even deeper form that shows us the love of the Creator. It is the Light that shines on us, even though we do not deserve it. Even in our unmet potential or in complete selfishness, still the Light of *Or Makif* shines on us. How does this concept work? How do we receive it if we don't deserve it? It doesn't make any sense! Either we deserve the Light or we don't. It doesn't fit in any of the laws of which Rav Ashlag or the Ari speak.

This illustrates what is such a beautiful secret about the nature of the Creator. The Creator cannot help Himself from sharing with us – He loves us too much! The Creator knows if He gave us everything, we would enjoy it so much, we would choose not to be selfless. So, He agrees to allow us to earn the Light. But He still gives us a gift from the perfection of the Endless World. Although there is now a barrier between us and the Light in this reality, the rules of our world do not apply to the *Or Makif* – it is from the world beyond. The *Or Makif* is more than just an incredible blessing. It is a sign of the great depth of the Creator's love for us.

The *Or Makif* manifests many ways in our lives. Every once in a while, we have these moments of realization. We know that an understanding or feeling we experience is not something we have earned, but is something from beyond. That is the *Or Makif*.

An example of this is the feeling of inspiration we get when we begin our spiritual work. You may notice that often people are excited when they first start studying spirituality. After a while, the real work starts, and then they lose that excitement - they start dropping off and stop growing. When a person begins his or her spiritual work, the Creator shines to him Light he doesn't deserve from the *Or Makif*. It is a powerful taste of the Endless World.

But that feeling of excitement *can't* last. Why? Because it is not coming from something they've earned. It is the shining of the *Or Makif*. Still, the *Or Makif* is so necessary to our process, because without it, we have no hope, especially in the beginning of our work. It is the driver of our change – it motivates us to transform.

It is almost comical to think that we had this great idea in the Endless World that we were going to cut ourselves off from the Light of the Creator in order to earn the Light. It would never have worked without the *Or Makif*! Without the *Or Makif* giving us a taste of the Endless World, we would never awaken our desire to receive the Light. The plan was so flawed that without the Creator's abundance of love, we would not be able to transform.

This should give us an incredible appreciation of the *Or Makif*. Every time we have an understanding or connection that is beyond us, we must thank the Creator for shining the Light of the *Or Makif* upon us, because we do not deserve it! It is a gift that the Creator slipped into this whole process of transformation. This is the beauty of this concept. It shows us the unconditional love of the Creator."

Show us Your kindness, O Eternal, and grant Your deliverance. I will hear what G-d, the Eternal will speak.

For He will speak peace to His people and His kind ones, they shall not return to foolishness.

Surely His deliverance is near to those who are in awe of Him, that glory may dwell in our land.

Kindness and truth have come together; justice and peace have kissed each other.

Truth will sprout from the earth, and justice will look down from heaven (Psalms 85:8-1).

Between Man and Woman

In *Jewish Meditation,* Rabbi Aryeh Kaplan includes in it a description of the wonderful ability that G-d has endowed us with to experience heaven touching earth in our intimate relationships with our mates:

"Although we usually refer to G-d as a male, in His true essence He is without gender. We refer to Him as a male, however, because we want Him to act upon the world through the male force of providence. We then leave ourselves open to G-d's providence, as a female is open to her mate.

The expression "the Holy One, blessed be He" is in the male gender and is therefore seen as denoting the male force of providence. It also relates to the *vav* of the Tetragrammaton. The Hebrew word for "Divine Presence," on the other hand, is *Shekhinah,* which is a feminine noun. The *Shekhinah* denotes the final *heh* in the divine name as well as the female power of providence.

It is significant that the Torah presents man and woman together as comprising the image of the Divine. The Torah thus says, "G-d created man in His image, in the image of G-d He created him, male and female He created them" (Gen. 1:27). This clearly implies that male and female together form the "image of G-d."

The reason for this is obvious. A male and female have the power to do the most G-dlike thing possible, namely, to create life. The power to conceive a child is so G-dlike that the Talmud states that when man and woman create a child, G-d Himself is their third partner.

Therefore, a husband and wife should see each other as being a reflection of the Divine. When a woman looks at her husband, she should see him as a reflection of "the Holy One, blessed be He," the male aspect of the Divine. Similarly, when a husband looks at his wife, he should see her as the Divine Presence *(Shekhinah),* the feminine aspect of the Divine.

When a person attains this goal, he will fully appreciate his wife's beauty and see it as a reflection of the Divine. He will then also be aware of her inner beauty, which is a reflection of the beauty of the *Shekhinah*. When one can contemplate this, one is filled with a love toward one's spouse that parallels the supernal love between the masculine and feminine forces of the Divine.

The Torah tells about the love between Jacob and Rachel, and describes it as one of the greatest loves the world has ever seen. It tells how Jacob was willing to work as an indentured servant for seven years to win Rachel's hand, and how the seven years "passed like days, so much did he love her" (Gen. 29:20). The Jewish mystics explain that Jacob saw himself as the male aspect of the Divine and Rachel as the female aspect; he therefore had a love that was a counterpart of the love on high.

When one is looking for a spiritual master, the first thing to examine is the master's relationship with his wife. From the way a man treats his wife, one can know how he relates to the *Shekhinah*. No matter how deep the master's meditations seem to be, no matter how wise his words, if he does not have a good relationship with his wife, then there is something missing from his spirituality. Conversely, when a man has a good relationship with his wife, even in the face of temptation and adversity, it is a clear indication that he is on a high spiritual level.

It is also significant that there is no encouragement of celibacy in the Jewish tradition, mystical or otherwise. Moses, the greatest of all mystics and prophets, was married, as were all the prophets and sages. Sex is seen not as a weakness of the flesh or as a necessary evil, but as a means to drawing close to G-d on a most intimate level.

When man and wife see each other as personifications of the divine image, then the sexual act becomes something holy. It is nothing less than the coming together of the male and female forces of creation. On a physical level, this has the power to create a child, but these forces parallel those on high which brought all creation into existence."

Therefore, when husband and wife are intimate, a man can see himself as being filled with the male aspect of the Divine, making an intimate connection with the female aspect. Similarly, a woman can see herself as the female aspect, receiving the male aspect. They can both realize that through their union, they are creating an "image of G-d."

For this to be accomplished, it is very important to avoid any extraneous thoughts during the sexual act. Partners should not think of any member of the opposite sex other than the sexual partner of the moment. As in any meditation involving action, concentration should be totally on the act itself, with all extraneous thoughts gently pushed aside.

There are several guidelines that are found in the Talmud and Kabbalah to enhance the meditative aspects of the act. First, the experience is meant to be primarily tactile, involving the sense of touch. Therefore, it should be performed in a room as dark as possible. Each party should have nothing distracting him or her from the experience.

G-d created the sexual act as one of the greatest pleasures that a human being can experience. For one thing, the act had to be pleasurable so that human beings would be drawn to it and thus perpetuate the species. But on a much deeper level, it is so great a pleasure because it allows man and woman together to emulate the Divine. When a man and woman experience pleasure from each other, they can contemplate this pleasure as a meditative experience. This will have the immediate effect of enhancing the pleasure many fold. If they see this pleasure as a gift of G-d, they will have great joy from it and, at the same time, experience a feeling of thanksgiving. On a deeper level, they can be aware of the spark of the Divine in the pleasure itself and elevate it to its source.

If a couple has such intentions, then the sexual act can be something holy. The Torah says that a married man may not "diminish his wife's conjugal rights" (Exod. 21:10). The Talmud interprets this to mean that it is one of the divine commandments that a husband and wife be intimate at regular intervals. Therefore, when being intimate, a husband and wife can also meditate on the fact that they are fulfilling one of G-d's commandments. Sex is not simply a mundane act that is being elevated, but a sacred act in its own right.

Very important in making sex a holy act is keeping the rules of family purity. This involves the woman's counting seven clays after the end of her period and then immersing in a *mikveh* (ritual bath). The monthly menses are seen as a cleansing process, and immersion in the *mikveh* as a process of rebirth. In many ways, immersion in the *mikveh* is more important to making sex a holy act than even marriage itself.

In general, using meditative techniques during intimacy can enhance the pleasure immeasurably. Such a practice focuses the minds of both partners exclusively on their mates and thus serves to strengthen the marriage bond. Couples who regularly use meditative techniques during intimacy have experienced important gains in their feelings toward each other. Couples who were experiencing marital difficulties found that when their sex life was sanctified, their love grew and other problems seemed to become inconsequential.

The type of meditation that a couple can do when they wish to conceive a child is somewhat different. This is because if they are on a certain level of consciousness, the thoughts that they have during intimacy can have a strong effect on the child conceived.

For many people, sex is associated with guilt and shame. But if we understand that G-d gave us sexual pleasure as a gift, we will realize that we can enjoy it to the fullest. Of course, sex is also an area of great temptation. A person may have committed sexual acts, such as adultery, which are regarded as sinful. Here, too, one must realize that sins can be repented; as the Talmud states, "Nothing can stand before repentance." Even if one has fallen into temptation, one can ask, with all one's heart, for G-d's forgiveness. The fact that a person may have sinned or done wrong need not diminish or destroy his or her ability to experience the Divine

Judaism views the sexual act as something very holy. It is a means through which a person can experience great intimacy with G-d. Judaism surrounds the sexual act with many rules and prohibitions, not because it views sex as something dirty or shameful, but because it views sex as something so holy that it must not be misused. Used correctly, with the right intentions and thoughts, sex can be the purest and holiest experience in the world, and meditation can enhance this aspect of the experience."

The Return of Prophecy

It may be that the long awaited return of prophecy is something that we will witness very soon, or maybe we will have to wait some more, but it is surely not premature to talk about the real possibility of seeing it happen in our days.

Over 800 years ago, the Rambam (Maimonides) wrote about his belief that the return of prophecy was imminent in his famous Letter to Yemen (Iggeret Teiman), where he wrote:

"The exact date of the coming of Mashiach cannot be known. But I have in my possession a great and amazing tradition that I received from my father and his grandfather, going back to our ancestors who went into exile at the time of the destruction of Jerusalem. As it says, 'and the exiles of Jerusalem that are in Spain' (Obadiah 1:20).

"This tradition is that Bilaam's sayings contain a hint of the restoration of prophecy in Israel. There are many instances where a verse in the Torah in addition to its simple meaning, also contains an allusion to something else. For example, we find that Jacob speaking to his sons said, 'R'du – Go down there [to Egypt]' (Genesis 42:2). R'du has the numeric value of 210, which is an allusion to the 210 years the Children of Israel would be exiled in Egypt. So too, venoshantem in the verse, 'When you have children, venoshantem – and have been established for a long time in the land...' (Deuteronomy 4:25), foretells in a hidden way how long the Jewish people would live in the Land of Israel. From the time they entered the land until the exile in the days of Jehoiakim is a total of 840 years. This is the numeric value of venoshtanem. Many similar examples can be cited.

"The family tradition that I received is based on this system of scriptural interpretation (by means of remez – hidden allusion). The tradition is based on Bilaam's oracle, 'Ka'eit' - at this point in time - it is said of Jacob and of Israel: 'What G-d is doing' (Numbers 23:23). This contains a concealed allusion regarding the restoration of prophecy in Israel. (Based on another tradition that ka'eit which means "equal in time") the verse means that after the passage of a period equal to the time elapsed since the six days of Creation, prophecy would be restored in Israel. Prophets will once again foretell 'what G-d is doing'. Bilaam made this prediction in the fortieth year after the Exodus, which was the year 2488 of Creation. According to this equation, prophecy will be restored in Israel in the year (1216 CE) 4976 of Creation (2 x 2488). (It should be remembered that the Rambam wrote this letter in 1172 CE). It is true beyond doubt that the restoration of prophecy is the first phase of the coming of Mashiach. As it is stated 'After that I will pour out My spirit on all flesh; your sons and daughters shall prophesy' (Joel 3:1).

"This is the most dependable of all the calculations that have been made about the coming of Mashiach. Although I have spoken out against making such calculations and strongly opposed the publicizing of the date of his arrival, I have done this in order to keep people from (falling into despair), thinking that his coming is in the distant future. I have mentioned this to you earlier. Blessed is HaShem Who knows the truth."

FROM A RECENT PROSPECTUS OF THE TEMPLE INSTITUTE IN JERUSALEM ON A PROPOSED COURSE ON THE RETURN OF PROPHECY

True prophecy once existed. A direct, or what can be called a vertical connection with heaven once existed. It once existed and it will exist again. And in a subtle way, not as outright prophecy, but within the mind and heart of every human being, it actually exists now.

As we shall see, our job is to refine ourselves to the point where that "still small voice" that almost no one hears presently, will break forth not only in the minds and hearts of select individuals (as in former times), but far beyond that, to a quantum leap in consciousness for all mankind. This is what is needed now. This is what HaShem, G-d, has said He will do. This is what we should be preparing for now.

Part of that preparation is **understanding what it entails, what prophecy is, according to the Torah, the prophets, and the sages**. As with many things that HaShem says, whether it involves a commandment in the Torah or a prophecy about the future, if HaShem says that He wants something, it is up to us to want it also. And if this idea of wanting what G-d wants is not clear, how to do it, etc. we will explain how it works.

So the Return of Prophecy is a magnificent subject. The fact that prophecy once existed, and that we are promised that it will exist again, this is actually all part of a great plan, the Creator's plan for mankind.

For instance, Adam and Eve were prophets. Not only did they hear G-d's voice, but their relationship with all creation was far different than anything we can imagine. If you imagine the Torah as a play or a movie, the first scene ends, the curtain falls, right after Adam and Eve are banished from Eden. The rest of the Torah is about how to get back in.

When Adam was in Eden, he was connected to all creation. There was only one thing he lacked. Himself. He was connected to the All so deeply that he lacked a solid sense of self. What he got from eating of the *Etz Daat Tov veRa* was himself, but in the process he lost that incredible connection he had had! This is what is meant about the curtain falling at the end of the first act, and that the remainder of the Torah is about getting back in to Eden with our Self.

As has been said, in Eden, Adam and Eve were prophets. What does this really mean? What is it like to be a prophet?
In Zohar Bereishit (1:31b) we read:

> Rabbi Yossi said... It is written, "*Elokim* said: 'Let there be light' and there was light. *Elokim* saw the light—that it was good—and *Elokim* made a division [separated] between the light and the darkness" (Genesis 1:3-4). This refers to the first light that the Holy One created. It is called the light of the eye [the light of consciousness]. It is the light that the Holy One showed Adam, with which Adam was able to see from one end of the universe to the other. It is the light that He showed David, concerning which David praised Him saying, "How great is the good [i.e., the light] that You have hidden away for those who revere You..." (Psalms 31:20). It is the light that He showed Moshe, with which he saw from Gilead to Dan [and the whole future of his people].

When the Holy One foresaw the three wicked generations—the generation of Enosh, the generation of the flood, and the generation of the tower of Babel—He hid this light away so that they would not have access to it [and misuse it]...

Seeing from one end of the universe to the other is to be understood both horizontally and vertically. That is, it certainly shone from east to west and from north to south. More importantly, it shone from above to below, from heavenly transcendence into earthly immanence. In addition, it means that Adam saw from the beginning of time to the end of time.

What was this light that Adam saw? What is G-d's light? We can best answer this by calling it a mental or spiritual light. It was the primordial light of G-d's presence permeating all worlds and everything in them. With this mental light Adam could close his eyes and know G-d. He could also enter into and explore any creature or any thing from the inside—a stone, an ocean, a cloud, a tree, a flower, an animal—and know its G-dly essence. He could concentrate his mind (and he was Mind) on anything, enter into it, and know it intimately.

In truth Adam was an angelic being sent down into the Garden of Eden in order to perform an awesome task that would have repercussions on the entirety of creation. The exalted level on which Adam and Eve existed is beyond anything we can imagine. Not only could they see "from one end of the universe to the other," but their molecular structure was different. Thus their bodies were not physical. They were pure light. And their ability to grasp truth and reality was equally different. They were so connected to the source of life that they could close their eyes and travel into other dimensions. Their ability to know G-d and experience His presence was awesome. There are beautiful sources for everything I am telling you. I want to share these sources with you.

In his masterful commentary to the Torah, Rabbi Moshe Alshikh (1521-1600) shows how Adam and Eve were initially dressed in garments of light. Their bodies were subtle and light, energy-bodies. Only afterwards did they become physical—skin, flesh, and bone.

147

In his commentary to the Zohar's *Sifra d'Tzeniuta* (Book of Concealed Mysteries), the Gaon of Vilna (Rabbi Eliyahu ben Shlomo Zalman, 1720-1798) states, "Adam was originally clothed in garments of light, referring to none other than the primordial hidden light. Only afterwards was he covered with skin, causing the light to be concealed."

The source for all these statements is the Zohar Pekudey (2:229b).

> Come see. When Adam was in the Garden of Eden, he was dressed in spiritual garments [i.e., his body was made] of supernal light. Once he was expelled from the garden, however, he required garments more fitting for this world. It is thus written, "G-d made garments of עור (animal skin) for Adam and his wife, and He clothed them" (Genesis 3:21).

> Prior to this, they were clothed in garments [i.e., their bodies were made] of אור, the light of that supernal radiance with which he perceived all the spiritual worlds when he was in the Garden of Eden.

> For it is known that the light of the Garden of Eden [did not come from the sun; rather, it] came from the supernal radiance. For this reason, when the Holy One placed Adam in the garden, He clothed him in garments [i.e., gave him a body] of light appropriate for that place. Without such garments he could not have existed there.

What is the Return of Prophecy? It is the Torah's prophetic story of how we lost Eden, with a built-in map of how to get back at a higher level than if we had never left. The Torah, in other words, is the repository, the heavenly safe-deposit box, of Edenic consciousness. No matter how distant we take ourselves and the world away from Eden, with the Torah we can always come back. This is certainly true about the prophetic level of the Torah, not only its prophetic teachings, but the spirit of prophecy that is alive within it. Through this hidden level of the Torah, we reconnect with Eden.

In other words, why does the Torah describe the descent of mankind as it does — the devolution of human consciousness that occurred after Adam and Eve lost Eden? So that we can understand the way back. The Torah is definitely not talking about retrograding backwards. It is very future oriented. Part of our course will be called Visions of the Future, through the eyes of the Prophets and the Great Master Sages.

And the idea is that learning about these things in this way, we will prepare and refine ourselves for that moment when the spirit of prophecy will break forth not only in the minds and hearts of select individuals (as in former times), but far beyond that, to a quantum leap in consciousness for all mankind.

So our purpose here is to reintroduce the concept of prophecy, or all the incredibly rich ideas that make up the concept of prophecy.

This is not a university course. It is rather a universe course, a course in what the universe is about, what prophecy teaches us about the universe, about the Creator of the universe, and our relationship to Him. It is also a universal course. We will take the purest teachings of the Torah and the Prophets, and show how they apply universally to all mankind and to each and every individual.

We will thus taste our first taste of prophecy, which is to wake up from the lower level of consciousness that characterizes earth life, wherein each nation lives its own myth irrespective of the larger reality of which we are all part.

Through true prophecy, on the other hand, we see that there are universal laws that apply across the board. These universal laws are hidden and therefore not understood. Mankind's fall from this clear understanding is what prophecy explains. The return of prophecy is the return to this deeper understanding.

Excerpt from the talk given by the Lubavitcher Rebbe of blessed memory on the eve of 28th Nissan, 5751 (1991)

What more can I do to motivate the entire Jewish people to clamor and cry out, and thus actually bring about the coming of *Mashiach*? All that has been done until now has been to no avail. For we are still in exile; moreover we are in an inner exile in regard to our own service of G-d.

All that I can do is to give the matter over to you. Now, **do everything you can to bring *Mashiach*, here and now, immediately. Act with all the energy and power of the lights of *Tohu,* but have your deeds balanced with the stability of the *keilim* of *Tikkun.***

May it be G-d's will that ultimately ten Jews will be found who are stubborn enough to resolve to secure G-d's consent to actually bring about the true Redemption, here and now immediately. Their stubborn resolve will surely evoke G-d's favour, as reflected by the interpretation of the verse, "for [i.e., *because*] they are a stiff-necked people; You will pardon our sins and wrongdoings and make us Your possession."

As a further effort, on my part to encourage and hasten the coming of the redemption, I will distribute money to each one of you with the intent that you give *tzedekah*, for "*Tzedekah* is great since it brings the redemption near."

I have done whatever I can; from now on, you must do whatever you can. May it be G-d's will that there will be one, two, or three among you who will appreciate what needs to be done and how it needs to be done, and may you actually be successful and bring about the true and complete redemption. May this take place immediately, in a spirit of happiness and with gladness of heart.

PEACE

In *The Garden of Peace*, Rabbi Shalom Arush explains that for peace to reign in the world, it must first be attained and maintained in our homes:

"A peaceful home surpasses any imaginable paradise. Those who live in a peaceful home have the feeling that they're walking around in an exotic garden of peace. Unfortunately, the opposite is true as well. Purgatory is a kindergarten compared to a home of marital strife. Living in a home environment that's devoid of peace is most likely life's worst form of tribulation.

The entire *Geulah*, or full redemption of our people, depends on peace in the home. A peaceful home is a worthy sanctuary for the *Shekhinah*, or Divine Presence. The more the Divine Presence fills this world, the closer we get to the *Geulah*. Therefore, every family that builds a peaceful home hastens the *Geulah*. Our sages say that peace is the best vessel there is for all kinds of blessings. By enhancing the peace in one's home, one merits every imaginable blessing. For that reason, it's worth making every effort to make our homes more peaceful."

In 1896, Theodor Herzl published *The Jewish State,* and the following year the First Zionist Congress was held in Basle, which prompted Ahad Ha'am (Asher Ginsberg), blessed with great understanding and prophetic insight, to write this:

"After thousands of years of unfathomable calamity and misfortune, it would be impossible for the Jewish people to be happy with their lot if in the end they would reach (merely) the level of a small and humble people, whose state is a plaything of its mighty neighbors and exists only by means of diplomatic machinations and perpetual submission to whomever fate is smiling upon. It would be impossible for an ancient people, one that was a light unto the nations, to be satisfied with such an insignificant recompense for all their hardships. Many other peoples, lacking both name and culture, have been able to attain the same thing within a brief period of time without having to suffer even the smallest part of what the Jews have suffered. It was not in vain that the prophets rose to the aid of Israel, envisioning the reign of *justice* in the world at the end of days. Their **nationalism**, their love for their people and for their land, led them to this. For even in biblical times the Jewish state was caught between two lions – Assyria or Babylon on the one side and Egypt on the other – so that it had no hope to dwell in tranquillity and develop in a suitable fashion. Accordingly, 'Zionism' developed in the hearts of the prophets, giving rise to the great vision of the end of days when 'the wolf shall dwell with the lamb and nation shall not lift up sword against nation' (Isaiah 2:4,6) – and when Israel shall dwell in its own land. Hence, this **human** ideal was an integral part of the **national** ideal of the Jewish people. The Jewish state can only find peace when universal justice will ascend to the throne and rule the lives of the peoples and the states."

Peace is such an indescribably lofty state of being, which we can begin to understand somewhat better when given the knowledge that Peace – Shalom is actually one of the names of G-d. Rabbi Shlomo Carlebach points to its holy nature in his own special way:

"Evil talk, even just hearing it, is the beginning of all hatred among people and wars among the nations.

The world would really like to have peace, but they don't know what it is, and they don't know how to get it. Imagine, you go into a hardware shop to buy ice-cream. They won't have it, right? People would love to have peace, but they are always going to the wrong store. They talk to the wrong people about it.

Peace between people is not something you can work on. It's a gift, the highest gift there is from Heaven. Peace is the greatest light that can shine from Heaven. I can ask G-d, 'Please make me well, and healthy, and rich, and give me everything in the world.' It is possible that one person, should be sick, G-d forbid, and another one well, because health and riches come from a place where they can be given to an individual.

Peace comes from such a high place that is not given to one person. I can't say to G-d, 'Please give me peace. The rest of the world I don't care about.' Peace has to be between me and the world, and between me and people, and between me and somebody else. Peace comes from the highest place there is, that holy place where the whole world is one.

You know my friends, peace is not going to come from the peace negotiators or the politicians. Only the common people, schleppers and thieves are the ones who can make peace. Our leaders are too busy talking about peace to have the time to really do something about it. In order to make peace you have to use your arms and your legs.

In one corner of the world a parent wakes up full of anger and yells at a child. The child goes to school full of anger and the negative vibrations continue. In another corner of the world, a happy parent greets a child in the morning with a loving kiss. The child goes to school infused with love and joy and a stream of peace flows forth. Generating the currents of peace is therefore a task that every human being can perform all day long.

Peace begins at home.

Sadly, sadly enough, most children do not have parents who tell them how special and beautiful they are. A girl once told me that when she gets back home her mother serves her breakfast by telling her how bad she is now. And for dinner, her mother turns prophetic and tells her how bad she will be in the future. You know, G-d could wake us up every morning with a thunderclap and tell us all He did and is going to do for us and then criticize everything we did wrong.

A husband madly in love with his wife and a wife madly in love with her husband are both teaching their children what love is. Children raised in love will not grow up to kill people and make war. They will not have to negotiate peace – they will live peace.

You know why there is no peace in the world? Because there is no true joy in the world. Imagine. My arch-enemy. My whole life I am searching for him to kill him in the most brutal way I know how. But I can't find him. So I go along with life with my wife and my two daughters. What can I do? Then one day G-d blesses me and I marry off my elder daughter. Well at the wedding I dance with all my energy. My joy is to seventh heaven. I get up on the table and dance with her. Suddenly, the door opens and in walks my arch-enemy. I quickly jump down and grab him. I say to him, 'Where were you? I've been waiting all my life to dance with you.' I grab him and lift him up to the table and I am dancing with my worst arch-enemy. My daughter's joy, my friend's joy brings peace to the world. Not some sad politicians negotiating. The world needs happy people to speak joyously with each other.

Then there is peace."

A NEW SONG

PSALM 33

1. Sing joyously to the Eternal, you righteous ones; it is fitting for the upright to offer praise.

2. Extol the Eternal with a harp; sing to Him with a ten-stringed lyre.

3. **Sing to Him a new song**; play well with sounds of jubilation.

4. For the word of the Eternal is just; all His deeds are done in faithfulness.

5. He loves righteousness and justice; the kindness of the Eternal fills the earth.

6. By the word of the Eternal the heavens were made, and by the breath of His mouth all their hosts.

7. He gathers the waters of the sea like a mound; He places the deep waters in vaults.

8. Let all the earth fear the Eternal; let all the inhabitants of the world tremble before Him.

9. For He spoke, and it came to be; He commanded, and it endured.

10. The Eternal has annulled the counsel of nations; He has foiled the schemes of peoples.

11. The counsel of the Eternal stands forever, the thoughts of His heart throughout all generations.

12. Fortunate is the nation whose G-d is the Eternal, the people He chose as a heritage for Himself.

13. The Eternal looks down from heaven; He beholds all mankind.

14. From His dwelling-place He looks intently upon all the inhabitants of the earth.

15. It is He Who fashions the hearts of them all, Who perceives all their actions.

16. The king is not saved by a great army, nor a warrior rescued by great might.

17. The horse is a false guarantee for victory; with all its great strength it offers no escape.

18. But the eye of the Eternal is directed toward those who fear Him, toward those who hope for His kindness,

19. to save their soul from death and to sustain them during famine.

20. Our soul yearns for the Eternal; He is our help and our shield.

21. For our heart shall rejoice in Him, for we have put our trust in His Holy Name.

22. May Your kindness, O Eternal, be upon us, as we have placed our hope in You.

PSALM 40

1. For the Conductor, a psalm by David.

2. I put my hope in the Eternal; He turned to me and heard my cry.

3. He raised me from the turbulent pit, from the slimy mud, and set my feet upon a rock, steadying my steps.

4. **He put a new song in my mouth**, a hymn to our G-d; multitudes will see and fear, and will trust in the Eternal.

5. Fortunate is the man who has made the Eternal his trust, and did not turn to the haughty, nor to those who stray after falsehood.

6. Many things have You done, You, O Eternal my G-d, Your wonders and thoughts are for us; none can compare to You; should I relate or speak of them, they are too numerous to recount!

7. You desired neither sacrifice nor meal-offering, but [obedient] ears You opened for me; You requested neither burnt-offering nor sin-offering.

8. Then I said, "Behold, I come with a Scroll of the Book written for me."

9. I desire to fulfill Your will, my G-d; and Your Torah is in my innards.

10. I proclaimed [Your] righteousness in a vast congregation; behold I will not restrain my lips, O Eternal, You know!

11. I did not conceal Your righteousness within my heart; I declared Your faithfulness and deliverance; I did not hide Your kindness and truth from the vast congregation.

12. May You, O Eternal, not withhold Your mercies from me; may Your kindness and truth constantly guard me.

13. For countless evils surround me; my sins have overtaken me and I cannot see; they outnumber the hairs of my head, and my heart has abandoned me.

14. May it be Your will, O Eternal, to save me; O Eternal, hurry to my aid.

15. Let those who seek my life, to end it, be shamed and humiliated together; let those who desire my harm retreat and be disgraced.

16. Let those who say about me, "Aha! Aha!" be desolate, in return for their shaming [me].

17. Let all those who seek You exult and rejoice in You; let those who love Your deliverance always say, "Be exalted, O Eternal!"

18. As for me, I am poor and needy; my Lord will think of me. You are my help and my rescuer; my G-d, do not delay!

PSALM 96

1. **Sing to the Eternal a new song**; sing to the Eternal, all the earth.

2. Sing to the Eternal, bless His Name; proclaim His deliverance from day to day.

3. Recount His glory among the nations, His wonders among all the peoples.

4. For the Eternal is great and highly praised; He is awesome above all gods.

5. For all the gods of the nations are naught, but the Eternal made the heavens.

6. Majesty and splendor are before Him, might and beauty in His Sanctuary.

7. Render to the Eternal, O families of nations, render to the Eternal honor and might.

8. Render to the Eternal honor due to His Name; bring an offering and come to His courtyards.

9. Bow down to the Eternal in resplendent holiness; tremble before Him, all the earth.

10. Proclaim among the nations, "The Eternal reigns"; indeed, the world is firmly established that it shall not falter; He will judge the peoples with righteousness.

11. The heavens will rejoice, the earth will exult; the sea and its fullness will roar.

12. The fields and everything therein will jubilate; then all the trees of the forest will sing.

13. Before the Eternal [they shall rejoice], for He has come, for He has come to judge the earth; He will judge the world with justice, and the nations with His truth.

PSALM 98

1. A psalm. **Sing to the Eternal a new song,** for He has performed wonders; His right hand and holy arm have wrought deliverance for Him.

2. The Eternal has made known His salvation; He has revealed His justice before the eyes of the nations.

3. He has remembered His kindness and faithfulness to the House of Israel; all, from the farthest corners of the earth, witnessed the deliverance by our G-d.

4. Raise your voices in jubilation to the Eternal, all the earth; burst into joyous song and chanting.

5. Sing to the Eternal with a harp, with a harp and the sound of song.

6. With trumpets and the sound of the shofar, jubilate before the King, the Eternal.

7. The sea and its fullness will roar in joy, the earth and its inhabitants.

8. The rivers will clap their hands, the mountains will sing together.

9. [They will rejoice] before the Eternal, for He has come to judge the earth; He will judge the world with justice, and the nations with righteousness.

PSALM 144

1. By David. Blessed be the Eternal, my Rock, Who trains my hands for battle and my fingers for war.

2. My source of kindness and my fortress, my high tower and my rescuer, my shield, in Whom I take refuge; it is He Who makes my people submit to me.

3. O Eternal, what is man that You have recognized him; the son of a mortal, that You are mindful of him?

4. Man is like a breath; his days are like a passing shadow.

5. O Eternal, incline Your heavens and descend; touch the mountains and they will become vapor.

6. Flash one bolt of lightning and You will scatter them; send out Your arrows and You will confound them.

7. Stretch forth Your hands from on high, rescue me and deliver me out of many waters, from the hand of strangers,

8. whose mouth speaks deceit and whose right hand is a right hand of falsehood.

9. **G-d, I will sing a new song to You,** I will play to You upon a harp of ten strings.

10. He who gives victory to kings, He will rescue David, His servant, from the evil sword.

11. Rescue me and deliver me from the hand of strangers, whose mouth speaks deceit and whose right hand is a right hand of falsehood.

12. For our sons are like plants, brought up to manliness in their youth; our daughters are like cornerstones, fashioned after the fashion of a palace.

13. Our storehouses are full, overflowing with all manner of food; our sheep increase by the thousands, growing by the tens of thousands in our open fields.

14. Our leaders bear the heaviest burden; there is none who break through, nor is there bad report, nor outcry in our streets.

15. Happy is the nation for whom this is so. Happy is that nation whose G-d is the Eternal.

PSALM 149

1. **Halleluyah! Sing to the Eternal a new song,** [recount] His praise in the assembly of the pious.

2. Israel will rejoice in its Maker; the children of Zion will delight in their King.

3. They will praise His Name with dancing; they will sing to Him with the drum and harp.

4. For the Eternal desires His people; He will adorn the humble with salvation.

5. The pious will exult in glory; they will sing upon their beds.

6. The exaltation of G-d is in their throat, and a double-edged sword in their hand,

7. to bring retribution upon the nations, punishment upon the peoples;

8. to bind their kings with chains, and their nobles with iron fetters;

9. to execute upon them the prescribed judgment; it shall be a glory for all His pious ones. Halleluyah!

"Sing to the Eternal a new song, His praise from the end of the earth, those who go down to the sea and all that is therein, the islands and their inhabitants" (Isaiah 42:10).

"By Your light will we see light" (Psalms 36:10).

"O cause a new light to shine over Zion" (the morning liturgy).

The beginning of prayer services and the end of the era of prophecy

As we see written in the Torah, the completion of the building of the Second Temple, and the restoration of offering sacrifices (korbanot) there, occurred in the days of Ezra and Nehemiah. We also learn that Ezra and the Anshei Knesset Ha-Gedolah (Men of the Great Assembly) laid out the content and order of formal prayer services.

Yet, later on, after the new practice of the recitation of these prayers was put in place, it has long been explained to us that these prayers were to be in lieu of - instead of the Temple offerings.

So how can the formal recitation of prayers have been in place of the Temple service, when korbanot were still being offered at the same time as these new formal prayers were being said? We need to look into this.

We are also told that the days of prophecy, that was so prolific in Israel, ceased at this very time, just as these prayer services commenced. Why?

Could there possibly be a connection here between these two events?

The capacity to be receptive to sublime thoughts and to be able to have loving relationships, is a wonderful gift that G-d has bestowed upon us all. What is necessary in order for us to experience ever deeper and more enhanced perceptions of our higher self, is to divest ourselves of any self-doubt we may have had, and rid ourselves of all negativity that may have accrued to us. Then we can allow our souls to soar and access the blissful levels of consciousness that our Creator wishes us to discover.

Ultimately, it is in this way that we may move forward, closer to the point that, by the grace of the Almighty, we are granted glimpses of divinity, followed by the gift of Ruach HaKodesh (the Holy Spirit), as we welcome the arrival of the *Geulah Shleimah* – the complete redemption (of the world), and prophecy is once more restored to Israel.

"But the word is very near to you, in your mouth and in your heart, that you may do it" (Deuteronomy 30:14).

Maimonides and Rabbi Moshe Chaim Luzzatto clearly state that the Holy Spirit still falls upon those who have refined themselves enough to receive it, who find favor in G-d's eyes, even though the era of prophecy ceased about 2,500 years ago, after the institution of prayer services.

Although our forefathers Avraham, Yitzchak and Yaakov and all of our prophets had no need for formal prayers, as they were totally connected to, and in direct communication with G-d, nevertheless, the set holy prayer services proved essential in uniting the Jewish people, and vital in keeping the hope of renewed Jewish sovereignty alive throughout our long exile, through to the present day. Undoubtedly, heartfelt prayers are very dear to G-d, - "since you are precious in My sight..." (Isaiah 43:4).

Yet, with the dawning of the Messianic age, as we see many a biblical prophecy being fulfilled, is it not reasonable to ask whether these beautiful and holy prayers should still be obligatory, now that at long last we are returning to our home, to the Promised Land, Eretz Yisrael?

As well as the formal prayer services, there are a multitude of pathways that we can take to be tightly attached to G-d – being granted whatever degree of spiritual awareness of HaShem that our kind deeds, mitzvot, Torah study, devoted blessings, meditation and personal prayers merit.

In the same way that exercising the body helps keep us in peak physical condition, so too will regular spiritual work uncover our inner treasure.

Opening up our minds and hearts, enables us to see G-d's hand at work in everything – in nature, in science, in every daily event, and in all aspects of our lives and our relationships.

Jacob dreamt of his soul climbing that ladder all the way to heaven. Moses had the experience of the burning bush that wasn't consumed. The Children of Israel sensed the sublime experience of that shuddering mountain with thunder and lightning, a thick cloud and the sound of a very loud horn.

In each instance, we are being given hints of the heights of spiritual consciousness and divine self-awareness that G-d will endow us with and be ours, if we can only open ourselves up to being showered with such blessings.

If we genuinely want Mashiach now, isn't it time for us to learn that **"new song"** that King David and the prophet Isaiah speak about?

We are told that prophecy will be restored: "Behold, I am sending you Elijah the prophet before the arrival of the Day of the Lord, that great and awesome day (Malachi 4:5)."

As Joel informs us that all of Israel will ultimately be granted the gift of prophecy, the question of what is required of us to attain that elevated state is well worth asking. We surely need to pray to G-d to be worthy to receive these higher powers, and make every effort to purify ourselves.

A Greater Revelation

Our rich treasury of deeply penetrating Torah wisdom that has been so essential in its time, and our lifeline in the many years of exile, now needs to be augmented, and to a certain degree superseded by a new teaching, **a new song** for the Messianic Era, a joyous song that enables a raising of human consciousness, and the experiencing of ever deeper levels of connection with our Creator.

This latest revolution in the teaching of Torah - this greater revelation for our times, at the end of days, is completely rooted in the Torah, and has been repeatedly spoken about over the ages. It is precisely regarding this turn of events that our forefathers, prophets and sages had already envisioned, passionately yearned for, and foretold us about.

This greater revelation is spoken about in Ezekiel 37 -

v 22 ...and I will make one nation in the land, upon the mountains of Israel, and one king shall be king to them all...

v 24 And My servant David shall be king over them and they shall all have one shepherd, they shall also walk in My ordinances and observe My statutes and do them.

v 25 ...and David My servant shall be their prince forever.

V 28 And the nations shall know that I am the Lord that sanctifies Israel, when My sanctuary will be in the midst of them forever.

We hear an echo here of what is written in Exodus 25:8 "...build Me a sanctuary and I will dwell in them".

This is the source of the idea of visualizing your body as a temple, with your head being the holy of holies. It is here, in this inner sanctum, that you may experience the divine revelation of discovering the Youniverse.

Rebbe Nachman teaches:

"If you wish to experience the Hidden Light and gain an awareness of the mysteries of the Torah that will ultimately be revealed, you should engage in much meditation directed toward G-d.

"Judge everything you do to see if it is worthy and proper to act in such a manner before G-d who is constantly doing good for you. You will then sustain your words with judgment. You are bringing yourself to judgment, and you yourself are the judge of all your deeds.

"Through this you will be worthy of comprehending the mysteries of the Torah. You will thus experience the Hidden Light that will be revealed in the Ultimate Future."

In these days, G-d consciousness will be universal as prophesied by Jeremiah, "…and they shall teach no more every man his neighbor, and every man his brother, saying 'Know the Lord'; for they shall all know Me, from the least of them to the greatest of them…" (Jeremiah 31:33).

As Rabbi Aryeh Kaplan tells us at the end of *Meditation and the Bible:*

"Maimonides writes that prophecy will have to be restored before the coming of the Messiah. As we have seen however, prophecy does not occur automatically, but must be cultivated with extensive discipline, through very specific practices. Before the Messianic age, therefore, these practices will have to be revealed and taught. Only then will there be a fulfillment of the prophecy, where G-d said, 'After that, I will pour out My spirit on all flesh, and your sons and your daughters will prophesy, your old men will dream dreams, and your young men will see visions (Joel 3:1).' "

Every instance of inner awakening evokes a resultant elevation of G-d consciousness throughout the world with a vast multiplier effect, and as this awareness of the dawning of the Age of Mashiach spreads, these ripples of spiritual enlightenment increase until they become tidal waves of illumination.

What we are witnessing more and more is a pandemic of simchah – as all the people of the world, one by one, begin to discover their unique and previously hidden potential, managing to finally get out of their own individual Egypt, free to enter their own personal promised land of self-fulfillment, reaching ever greater spiritual heights. This joy is infectious!

It is in these wonderful times that we can look forward to seeing the evolvement of human consciousness to a new level of understanding, receiving the gift of a world at peace, enjoying the universal knowledge of G-d that the Hebrew prophets had foreseen and spoken about.

In this new era, mankind will truly become ManKind.

Every Time

To everything there is a season,

and a time to every purpose under the heaven;

a time to be born,	*and a time to die;*
a time to plant,	*and a time to pluck up that which is planted;*
a time to kill,	*and a time to heal;*
a time to break down,	*and a time to build up;*
a time to weep,	*and a time to dance;*
a time to mourn,	*and a time to laugh;*
a time to cast away stones,	*and a time to gather stones together;*
a time to embrace,	*and a time to refrain from embracing;*
a time to seek,	*and a time to lose;*
a time to keep,	*and a time to cast away;*
a time to rend,	*and a time to sew;*
a time to keep silence,	*and a time to speak;*
a time to love,	*and a time to hate;*
a time of war,	*and a time of peace;*

(Ecclesiastes 3:1-8)

- Every time you act kindly, the world has more kindness.
- Every time you are compassionate, the world has more compassion.
- Every time you smile to someone, the world is a more cheerful place.
- Every time you help transform someone's worry into serenity, the world is a more serene place.
- Every time you calm someone who is angry, the world is a more pleasant place.
- Every time you encourage someone to give money to charity, the world is a more charitable place.

- Every time you encourage someone to do something for others, you are creating a partner to make a better world.

Some people spend way too much time complaining about the awful state the world is in. There is too much aggression and violence. There is too little kindness and compassion. There is too much anger and depression and too little serenity and joy.

If someone complains and complains, the world is still full of whatever it is the person is complaining about, and now more complaining has been added. Conversely, if someone spreads compassion and kindness, the world improves. The ripple effect can spread these positive qualities. A little positive action is more beneficial than a mountain full of complaints.

- Every time you visit someone who is ill, you are making the world a kinder place to live in.
- Every time you comfort a mourner, you are making the world a kinder place to live in.
- Every time you judge someone favorably, you are making the world a kinder place to live in.
- Every time you lend one of your possessions to someone, you are making the world a kinder place to live in.
- Every time you help a stranger find his way, you are making the world a kinder place to live in.

What emerges from all this is that there is no such thing as an insignificant act, because every time you do an act of kindness you are elevating the world we live in.

RABBI ZELIG PLISKIN

Your hands have made me and fashioned me; grant me understanding, and I will learn Your commandments.

Those who fear You will see me and rejoice, for to your word have I aspired.

I have known, O Eternal, that Your laws are just; and in faithfulness did You afflict me.

May Your kindness comfort me, according to Your word to Your servant.

Let Your compassion come upon me, that I may live, for Your Torah is my delight.

Let the scoffers be shamed, for they have maligned me with falsehood; but I will meditate upon Your precepts.

May they return to me - those who fear You, and those who know Your testimonies.

May my heart be perfect in Your statutes, so that I not be shamed.

(Psalms 119:73-80)

"And I will return the captives of My people Israel, and they shall build the waste cities, and inhabit them; and they shall plant vineyards, and drink the wine from them; they shall also make gardens and eat of their fruit" (Amos 9:14).

"After that, I will pour out My spirit on all flesh; and your sons and your daughters shall prophesy, your old men shall dream dreams, your young men shall see visions" (Joel 3:1).

If you enjoyed reading *ManKind* and found it illuminating, please go to its Amazon page at www.amazon.com/dp/0995656002 and give your review of the book and the amount of stars (1-5) that you believe it deserves.

The more five star reviews *ManKind* receives, the higher visibility the book will be given on the internet, and the greater the likelihood that more people will also have the opportunity of being able to buy the book and be inspired and enlightened by it.

A wonderful way for as many people as possible to also have the benefit of reading this book, is if you become a reseller of *ManKind* and at the same time earn extra money, by buying discounted copies and selling them on.

If you want to become one of our resellers, this is very easy to arrange (free shipping on all orders).

For orders of 10-99 books the cost to you is $9.50 for each book.

For orders of 100+ books the cost to you is $7.00 for each book.

Send an email to promisedland920@gmail.com to place your order, giving your name and address, then make a payment by PayPal to our email address, confirming your name, and the details of your order, and we will then expedite the delivery of your order to you.

Nachum Shaw is the editor of *Torah for the Nations,*
A Healthy Future, The House on the Mountain,
Universal Torah and *Know Your Bible*;
all by Rabbi Avraham Greenbaum,
director of the *Azamra Institute* in Jerusalem.

These books are published by Promised Land
and are available to buy on Amazon.

www.ingramcontent.com/pod-product-compliance
Lightning Source LLC
LaVergne TN
LVHW011233080426
835509LV00005B/480